The
WORD

The
WORD

Black Writers Talk About
the *Transformative Power* of
Reading and Writing

INTERVIEWS
Edited and with an Introduction by
Marita Golden

Broadway Paperbacks • New York

Published in the United States by Broadway Paperbacks, an imprint of the
Crown Publishing Group, a division of Random House, Inc., New York.
www.crownpublishing.com

Broadway Paperbacks and its logo, a letter B bisected on the diagonal,
are trademarks of Random House, Inc.

Library of Congress Cataloging-in-Publication Data
The word : Black writers talk about the transformative power of
reading and writing : interviews / edited and with an introduction
by Marita Golden.
p. cm.
1. American literature—African American authors. 2. African
Americans—Literary collections. 3. African Americans—Intellectual life.
4. African American authors—Interviews. 5. Reading—United States.
6. Authorship—United States. I. Golden, Marita.

PS153.N5W67 2010
810.8'0896073—dc22
2010003391

ISBN 978-0-7679-2991-2
eISBN 978-0-307-72077-1

Printed in the United States of America

Book design by Lauren Dong
Cover design by Nupoor Gordon

10 9 8 7 6 5 4 3 2 1

First Edition

To Clyde McElevene, my friend and bibliophile par excellence,

who has generously nurtured my love of reading and books,

and whose passion for the word is singular and inspiring.

Thank you for making me a better reader, writer, and thinker.

Contents

The
WORD

Let's imagine there's an earthquake tomorrow in the average university town. If only two buildings remained intact at the end of the earthquake, what would they have to be in order to rebuild everything that had been lost? Number one would be the medical building, because you need that to help people survive, to heal injuries and sickness. The other building would be the library. All the other buildings are contained in that one. Reading is at the center of our lives. . . . Without the library you have no civilization.

—RAY BRADBURY

❊

If you open up scripture, the Gospel according to John starts: "In the beginning was the Word." Although this has a very particular meaning in Scripture, more broadly what it speaks to is the critical importance of language, of writing, of reading, of communication, of books as a means of transmitting culture and binding us together as a people.

—BARACK OBAMA, *then U.S. senator from Illinois speaking before the annual conference of the American Library Association, June 23, 2005*

Introduction

THIS IS A book about stories. An extended meditation in a choir of voices, all remembering and recounting how stories defined and made possible creativity, community, and a meaningful life. Reading and writing are the twin pillars of modern civilization, endeavors that exist as a kind of oxygen necessary for the transformation of both individuals and societies. Global in their potential impact, reading and writing are, however, among the most intimate, even secretive, acts we can perform.

Both are so deeply woven into our understanding of communication and reflection that we take them for granted, often unaware of the myriad gifts they render unto us. From both acts we gain self-knowledge, empathy, catharsis, information, and answers to questions we had not yet felt trembling on the margins of our dreams. We are launched into our next adventure, be it a journey to another land or a new job, because a book told us we could do it. We give our fantasies a dry run on the pages of a diary or in the words of fictional characters, each single word we write drawing us closer to what words have suddenly made quite chillingly real.

Books have marked some of the most important passages of my life and positioned me in continuous dialogue with strangers whose work influenced my values, mirrored my inner turmoil, provided me with delight and moments of bliss. There are stories we need that often only a book can tell.

※◇※

I AM huddled, as I often am as an adolescent, in the attic of our house. Seeking isolation. Alone time. *I am reading. Oliver Twist, Jane Eyre, Vanity Fair.* I am boisterous and shy, moody and misunderstood. But in the attic, none of that matters. Books are a magic carpet I ride to a place outside myself, into worlds seductively strange yet familiar. A classmate at school is as vain as *Vanity Fair*'s Becky Sharpe. I have felt in my bones Jane Eyre's self-doubt all too well. I have seen newspaper photos of children as poor as Oliver Twist. I tremble with anticipation each time I open a book. I smile with satisfaction when I read the last page.

※◇※

1968. I have discovered that Black people live in books and have done things momentous and historic in the world. Malcolm X, Martin Luther King, Jr., and Bobby Kennedy are dead, made martyrs by assassins' guns. My faith in America has been cremated and cast to the winds. In my grieving I turn to stories that complete the history barely begun in my classes at school. Slave revolts. W.E.B. DuBois, Timbuktu, Nat Turner. Bessie Smith. Ida B. Wells. Books turn me bitter, then they make me proud, and then they make me brave, putting flesh and blood on the bones of a past my Afrocentric father kindled for me in spurts. Books make me a Black Woman.

※◇※

I AM weeping, too distraught to continue. I cannot imagine actually completing the text. Halfway through *Beloved,* Toni Morrison's meditation on the price some of us will pay to be free, I am torn asunder. Speechless, I am utterly amazed by the terrible beauty and grandeur of this tale. My tears have been shed in Auschwitz, on the Middle Passage, by rape victims, men dying in trenches, and children lit by the fires of Hiroshima. Yet in the end, the tears leave me replenished, fortified with a courage I have never known. I open the book. I can bear anything.

※◇※

MY MARRIAGE has become a prison. I am seriously considering divorce and find myself reading *Madame Bovary,* Gustave Flaubert's ode to illusion, fleeting romance, marriage, and adultery. Because I love life much more than the novel's heroine Emma Bovary does, and I have a child to live for, unlike Emma, there will be no suicidal exit from my dilemma. Still, Emma Bovary knows more about me at this moment than anyone else. She alone knows the perimeters of the tomb my life has become. In this, my darkest hour, this fictional character is my best friend.

※◇※

EACH OF those books enlarged me. Growing up in Washington, D.C., in a close-knit African-American community, in the waning days of segregation, nineteenth-century British classics were my first international passport. While much of the history of African Americans had been marginalized by mainstream history books, a band of dedicated Black and White historians had, nonetheless, worked to fill in the missing pages of my and my country's complex, compelling story. *Beloved* plunged me into the deepest end of the ocean of our inhumanity toward one another and our redemptive impulses that manage, somehow, to ennoble our souls. Reading *Madame Bovary* as my life crumbled all around me was bracing and cautionary.

Reading has given me fluency in the language of sorrow, the grammar of grace, experiences that unite us across borders and time zones. Books feed and create our imagination. Flip the first page and you are whispering, "I am now in your hands." Finish a hundred pages and you have said, "Take me. I am yours." As an act of independence and independent thinking, reading a book has few rivals. At ten, walking through the hushed rooms of my neighborhood library, running my fingers across the spines of the texts lining the shelves, I approached the act of choosing just the right book to read as a nearly hallowed choice and opportunity. Already I knew reading was serious and sacred.

The stories the writers in this book recount as they remember their earliest reading and writing experiences are testimony to the power of books to inspire and call us to migrate, wander, and move through the world with the daring of an ancient explorer. The more we read with an open mind, the more our intellect demolishes artificial notions of "difference" among God's children. In actuality, we read with our bodies, our minds, and our souls. The act of reading is wholistic, leaving no aspect of our lives untouched or unchanged.

The symbiotic relationship between reading and writing is a cornerstone of our individual intellectual journeys and our educational system. We write as an act of self-expression. We read because language renders unto us the vitality of real and imagined experience.

We are in the midst of a national conversation that is often wrenching, full of indictment and hand wringing about the diminishing role of both reading and writing in our lives. Government studies, a whole new genre of books dedicated to the topic, articles in the mainstream press, and scholarly journals, blogs, and chat rooms all bemoan the decline in the reading and writing skills of young people and the assault on the habit of reading by new media, as well as the growing indifference to serious literature, and the decline of the bookstore as a cultural space of singular significance.

As this conversation has grown louder and more insistent, I have yearned to hear the voices of African-American writers as part of this dialogue. That is one reason I wanted to compile these interviews. This book is also inspired by my desire as the author of more than a dozen books to talk to other writers about the texts that made them lifelong readers, changed their ideas about the world, and made them want to be writers.

Under slavery it was illegal to teach Blacks how to read, and Whites considered literate Blacks subversive and dangerous. Even today there remains much intraracial joking about how "dangerous" (to the status quo) the sight of a young Black person reading is, but in this case the act of reading endangers the persistent (but unfounded) belief that Black people hardly read at all. In the face of a national dropout rate of 60 percent among African-American high school students, African-American youth need to know, now more than ever, that just as their ancestors died for the right to vote, they sometimes died for the right to read. A library is a constellation of possibilities; a sentence is the first step toward the tangible.

The crisis of confidence that plagues the Black community around the varying issues associated with educational achievement and literacy exists in the shadow of contemporary Black literary giants like playwright August Wilson, who has been for many years the most produced American playwright, a status unchanged by his death; Toni Morrison, who is arguably the most popular, high-profile, and read Nobel Prize winner of recent times; and Maya Angelou, who is considered a kind of literary national treasure. Despite the success of these writers, the complicated and enduring legacy of slavery and legal segregation, poverty, and racism has made attaining and holding on to gains in education a persistent challenge in the Black community. The current national discourse about literacy and literature is especially relevant to Black Americans. Our future as a people, our ability to sit at the table where the blueprints for tomorrow are drawn up means that this conversation is not just necessary; it is urgent.

Nearly a century and a half after the abolition of slavery, African-American achievement, access to economic mobility, and professional success are still determined, in large measure, by the type of education to which our communities have access. Without the ability to write a coherent outline of our desires, they remain wishful thinking. Without the wisdom gained through reading about how others made their dreams reality, we wander blindfolded and stumbling through the skeletal remains of all we hope to attain. The educational challenge Black students face is a mirror of the larger national educational crisis. A nation that is indifferent to the cultivation of imagination, is tolerant of increasing levels of functional illiteracy among its populous, and that fails to promote the quest for reason and truth through writing will not long endure.

This is the backdrop that frames the conversations in this book. These dialogues are not only stimulating and inspiring, they also provide guidelines for those intent on spreading the gospel of reading and writing as acts of importance.

My own love of reading is rooted in my parents' faith in the power of education. Neither my mother nor my father graduated from high school. They nevertheless became masters, in their own way, of their destinies. Both were driven and ambitious, and recognized the importance of educational attainment for me. My parents possessed the robust, unquenchable belief of the dispossessed in the ability of education to defeat marginalization, discrimination, and powerlessness.

Beatrice and Francis Golden believed education was the key to the best in oneself and the best of all that life had to offer. In this sense they were typical Americans. Some of the most important myths we have created as a nation center around self-made men and women using books to fashion a way into the world.

My mother didn't bring much book learning with her from Greensboro, North Carolina, when she migrated to Washington, D.C., as part of the Great Migration of Blacks from the South to northern cities that transformed this country in the 1920s and '30s. But her tireless mantra to me was "Get an education and no one can ever take it away from you." When I was fourteen she baptized me with my life's purpose by telling me as we stood at the kitchen table making biscuits that one day I was going to write books. In my sophomore year in college she bought me a subscription to the *New York Times*, and no gift was ever more cherished. I was her daydreaming, book-reading, poetry-writing, ten-syllable-word–spouting daughter and in my nascent literary expressions I am sure she saw the fulfillment of some measure of her own dreams.

My father drove a taxicab, had read Tolstoy and Jefferson, and seemed to know everything about Black history. A quintessential self-educated man, he told me bedtime stories about Harriet Tubman, Sojourner Truth, and Cleopatra. I learned to write by listening to those stories of larger-than-life heroes and heroines who changed themselves and everyone around them. I read, in part, because I knew my father had learned those stories on the pages of books.

More than any writing course, teacher, or mentor, I owe my passion for reading and writing to my parents. Their pride in what they saw these activities inspire me to do and be was an enormous boost to my sense of self.

Books still matter in this age in which individuals in our global community connect through the technological umbilical cord we call the Internet. We take for granted and remain amazed and entertained by a continuing stream of "new media" that moves us through our experiences and thoughts seemingly at "warp" speed. Even in this milieu of dramatic, daily evolution, books still matter. The seductions, innovations, and revolutionary changes brought forth by the computer chip do not erase the fact that the bound book remains one of the most convenient and impressive of technological inventions. It provides a private, intimate, sensual experience that results in expansion of the mind and enhancement of the soul. The book is an antidote to the breakneck pace that threatens to render meditation, reflection, deep thought, and pondering (all attributes of a meaningful reading experience) obsolete.

Books were "events" long before Harry Potter. And at its best, a book that readers come to treasure is a celebratory happening as extravagant as a Fourth of July fireworks display, as reassuring as a prayer.

The writers in this book share stories about the stories that have shaped them, comforted and challenged them, and connected them to the virgin territory within themselves and the echo of their desires in the hearts of others. Perhaps now as never before, books are a necessary lingua franca needed to blast through the walls of religion and tribe and first world and third world distance and dogma that we have erected. Books and reading connect us without the need for a passport. Books need no explanation, no justification. Books are so humble, so patient, and they ask only one thing: to be read, to allow them to enlarge our spirit and our possibilities. I have been accompanied through all my most important life passages by books. I am a wife, a mother, and a grandmother who, like the writers in this book, eagerly looks forward to the books waiting to be a part of the rest of my journey.

MARITA GOLDEN RECOMMENDS

War and Peace by Leo Tolstoy

Beloved by Toni Morrison

The Third Life of Grange Copeland by Alice Walker

The Kiss by Kathryn Harrison

Pride and Prejudice by Jane Austen

The Making of Black Revolutionaries by James Foreman

Part I

Reading Beyond Borders

"I believe that it's the duty of every truly free citizen to read, especially to read beyond your borders."

—Edwidge Danticat

FOR AFRICAN-AMERICAN READERS, SEEING AND DISCOVering themselves on the pages of books is a profoundly affirmative experience. The writers in these interviews recall the heady experience of confronting themselves as the beating heart of a narrative, not marginalized or rendered as a twice-told tale. Yet simultaneously, reading set them in motion, made them world citizens. Reading made them writers who traveled, who wandered beyond the borders of their neighborhoods. Reading and writing presented them with opportunities beyond even the most daring hopes their parents had for their lives.

Reading broadens the scope of the world and one's perception of where one belongs in it.

Books are a compass and all writing is in some ways a map. Passionate readers break the codes that often render experience indecipherable and writers build a highway that transports them literally through time and space, launched by the engine of curiosity and the vitality of language.

ELLIS COSE *is a respected and best-selling author, columnist and contributing editor for* NEWSWEEK, *and producer of the Public Radio International documentary series* AGAINST THE ODDS. *In* THE RAGE OF A PRIVILEGED CLASS, *Cose brilliantly examined the emotional price the African-American middle class pays in its pursuit of social equality and economic parity. The book laid bare the endurance of racism as a fact of life for even the most materially successful Blacks.* BONE TO PICK: OF FORGIVENESS, RECONCILIATION, REPARATION, AND REVENGE *is a wide-ranging look at a number of societies—the United States, Ghana, South Africa, and Peru among them—and their ways of coping with shared legacies of national cruelty and pain. And*

THE ENVY OF THE WORLD: ON BEING A BLACK MAN IN AMER-ICA *was featured on the cover of* NEWSWEEK *and inspired a special program produced by National Public Radio. Cose's other books include the novel* THE BEST DEFENSE, A NATION OF STRANG-ERS: PREJUDICE, POLITICS, AND THE POPULATING OF AMERICA, *and* COLOR-BLIND: SEEING BEYOND RACE IN A RACE-OBSESSED WORLD.

In his capacity as president of Ellis Cose, Inc., Cose produces AGAINST THE ODDS, *which profiles individuals around the world who have overcome tremendous adversity. The program airs on public broadcasting stations around the United States. Cose has appeared on* THE TODAY SHOW, DATELINE, ABC EVENING NEWS, *and* GOOD MORNING AMERICA *and has won many awards for his journalism.*

Ellis Cose has, with insatiable curiosity about the world and a commitment to seeking out and telling the hardest stories, enlightened and informed and challenged himself, his readers, and his listening audiences.

MARITA GOLDEN: What advice would you give to a young person starting out in journalism today?

ELLIS COSE: I would say that you really need to cultivate your curiosity. Journalism can take you lots of different places and have you talking to lots of different people about a whole variety of subjects and things. It's even more important, I think, to have a broad set of interests that will be able to serve you well as you talk to people from every walk of life and from various kinds of cultures.

MG: You've become a multimedia person, now branching out from journalism into writing books and producing a radio program and planning to move into television. But you began writing books at a pretty young age; how did you start?

EC: I got into my head, essentially when I was sixteen, that I wanted to be a writer. And so the first serious thing that I really tackled was trying to write a book that grew directly out of the riots in 1966 and 1968. There were two sets of riots in Chicago; one came in '66, which began with a police incident and then grew into a huge riot, which was my first experience with that.

MG: What was your neighborhood in Chicago?

EC: It was a West Side community called Henry Horner Housing Projects. Those housing projects no longer exist. But they were not too far from downtown Chicago. My family and I heard and saw gunfire going back and forth, and large parts of the community were torn up. That sort of repeated itself in '68 after the death of King. I was a witness to the coverage of the *Chicago Tribune* and how stereotypical it was, how it painted my community, how nonrepresentative it was. I wanted to respond to that.

MG: To put this in some perspective, describe your neighborhood.

EC: Honey, our neighborhood was the projects. By definition it was poor as you could get. I mean, there were certainly people who worked, and so it was working class, and welfare, and a combination of all those kinds of people who needed subsidized housing. And when we moved into the projects from the, quote, "ghetto," community, it was really a step up. I remember I was five when we moved into it, and I remember running around thinking it was like this palatial place.

MG: One of your teachers played a crucial role in your starting to write about all this, didn't she?

EC: My English teacher Mrs. Klinger and I had been having this ongoing battle about English. It was just a battle that I had with every English teacher in high school. And the battle essentially was I felt their assignments were boring, and uninteresting, and unchallenging, and I was pretty much refusing to do the work.

I attended Lane Technical. Lane was considered the best public school in Chicago and it was a school for the kids who were bright but who couldn't afford to go to private school. It had a sort of elite tradition. And if you could do well on standardized tests and you grew up in a certain area, you could go to Lane. And I always knew I was a bright kid. I had always tested extremely well even when I was in my so-called ghetto schools. I was always testing in the 98–99 percentile.

We were very poor, yet I always tested well. My parents, who were not terribly well educated themselves, were both products of the time when educating Black people was not at all a priority in the South, but despite this, my parents emphasized reading. And so we had library cards when we were very young.

At Lane, a lot of what we did consisted of reading passages and then answering questions about them, and I knew I knew the answers, and the questions didn't strike me as very interesting. So I just refused to do it.

So I had these perennial run-ins with my English teachers because of that.

By the time I was a senior I was totally fed up with English and English classes. I thought that's where people who weren't very interesting thinkers ended up.

MG: It didn't stretch you creatively or intellectually?

EC: Not at all. And so Mrs. Klinger called me one night at home. She was my last English teacher. She said to me, "Ellis, I know you can do the work because whenever you do it, it's fine, but you're not doing it, why?" I asked her, "Why don't you give me a research and writing assignment and I'll do something with that?" Of course the riots were on my mind, so I said, "Why don't I do a paper on riots and why they happened in my community, why they happened in America, what the history of all this is." And she said, "Well, fine, you go do that."

So all of a sudden for the first time in my high school experience I got excited about English and ended up turning in a 150-page essay that I worked on for several weeks, looking at the history of riots in America, race riots in different areas, in the community, and I was looking especially at Chicago. She took it home, and after the weekend she called me up after class and said, "Ellis, I'm going to give you an A in the course. But I'm not really capable of judging this material. I've taken a course with Gwendolyn Brooks, we'll send it to her. You know who she is, right?" I said, "Well, sort of. I mean, she's a poet laureate, whatever that is, I know that."

So I packed up this manuscript and sent it to her. In the

interim I had really gotten into my head that this writing thing wasn't bad at all, and I started work on a novel.

MG: What was it about that assignment that gave you so much satisfaction?

EC: It gave me a chance to express a lot of thoughts and ideas and feelings that I hadn't really had a medium to express these things in. Even though I had always had this sort of, for lack of a better word, contempt for the English classes I had been taking, I had from a very early age fallen in love with reading, which I had to do a lot of for that assignment.

MG: What books were you reading as an adolescent?

EC: I remember I must have been thirteen or fourteen when I read James Baldwin's *The Fire Next Time.* I think the first riots had taken place in Chicago. I remember that being a revelation to me, the fact that somebody thought about things that I had thought about and made connections to things that I felt needed connecting. I felt the same thing with *Invisible Man,* which I read when I was quite young.

I was hooked on reading as a child and never became unhooked. As a kid growing up on the West Side of Chicago, I had very little sense of the larger world beyond what I saw on television or discovered through reading. Even as a youngster, I always found the experience of reading about something much more satisfying than watching TV. There is something more profound and also more intimate in exploring a subject by reading about it. Reading has taken me in both a figurative and literal sense around the world. And it continues to open new horizons. Reading matters for one very simple reason.

There is no way to acquire deep knowledge without reading. It scarcely matters what the subject is, the gateway to knowledge is still the written word.

MG: What books have been most influential in your life and your work?

EC: *Invisible Man* by Ralph Ellison and *Crime and Punishment* by Dostoyevsky were both important books in terms of shaping my conceptions of writing, and of its power. I read *Invisible Man* when I was twelve or thirteen and remember being deeply moved not just by the story but by the beauty of the writing. I discovered *Crime and Punishment* when I was in high school and that book gave me insight into the power of fiction in communicating big ideas.

Reading has taken me in both a figurative and literal sense around the world. And it continues to open new horizons.

MG: So the writing really gave you a way to express things that you felt very deeply about. Reading worked in tandem with that and that was important.

EC: Oh yeah. At that point I, of course, had this dream that other people would read it, but it was also just an interesting way for me to learn how to express myself. So during the time when I was waiting for Gwendolyn Brooks to respond, and I had no idea what Gwendolyn Brooks would do, I started writing this novel; I haven't looked back at it in years, and I don't even know where it is, but it's about coming of age in the hood.

MG: I find when people say, well, I'm going to write a book, they have no idea how difficult it is to marshal the emotional and creative energies over the length of time required to write even a first draft of a novel. So when you say you were doing that at sixteen, that is really an extraordinary endeavor.

EC: I think my parents thought it was kind of weird that I was around the kitchen table, dining room table, writing, writing, and writing.

MG: Did you finish the novel?

EC: Well, between the ages of sixteen, seventeen, and nineteen I finished a couple of novels. Well, manuscripts. Actually I even got a contract for one of them, which ended up not being published for a variety of reasons. Gwendolyn Brooks ultimately called out of the blue one Saturday. She said to me, "Ellis, you have got to come and talk to me." And I said, "Okay, where?" And she gave me the name of the college, Northeastern Illinois State College, and it was like three bus rides away, I remember that. So it was like this long journey to see Gwendolyn Brooks.

I knew her books of course, but that's all. When I get to the school, she ushers me into her office, and she pulls out my manuscript. And she has scribbled across it in both red and blue ink, "One day you will be a great writer," which is characteristic of her generosity and spirit and her way of nurturing young people. But of course it made a huge impact on me. And she gives me what amounts to a lecture. She says, "I don't know what you're going to do, what you plan to do with your life, but you really should be writing because you have this gift." I was just sort of blown away. So she invites me to join her writers' group. That's where I met Dudley Randall, all these folks who were part of her group, Haki Madhubuti, who was Don Lee back then. You have to remember again I was seventeen I guess at the time. I went to a few of these writing groups, which, first of all, it was a bus ride to get to it. But, secondly, the thing I remember thinking was that I really don't have much in common with these folks because they were all in their thirties.

So I didn't stay in the writing group for very long. I ended up dropping out. But in the process I had met some of these people and gotten sort of more into this idea of writing.

MG: How did the writing group work, what was their process?

EC: I remember the process was that people would read things they were working on, and people would talk about it. They would talk about their projects. Sam Greenlee was working on *The Spook Who Sat By the Door*, and he came through there at one point even though he wasn't really in Chicago, and he talked about that. Haki was there with all his different poetry talking about what he was doing, and so was Carolyn Rogers.

Ms. Brooks just made it very clear she respected my talents. She was there to be helpful. She would be supportive, and I was very grateful for that. It was such a tremendous sort of thing knowing somebody who had validated me. I mean she was poet laureate of the state of Illinois. She had won the

Pulitzer. Yeah. So she was as major as it can get. And I continued writing.

I think it was my second novel, which I sent to Path Press. It was just a small group out of Chicago who decided to start a publishing company. They accepted the novel for publication and sent me a contract, and my mother had to sign it. But they never published a book. They could never put together the resources to do that.

I wrote one nonfiction book, two novels, and a bunch of essays, and none of them were published. The nonfiction book was the essay I had done for my course, then I did two, three novels. Then by this time I had graduated; I'm in college at the University of Illinois, Chicago campus.

I'm still sort of doing all this writing, and not finding any financial reward in it. And I decided that what I needed to do was to find a way that I could do my writing and also find a way to earn some money from it.

MG: Make writing pay.

EC: Yeah. I had been reading newspapers a lot. I had always read newspapers. And I remember there were columnists there who I would read, who talked about the news of the day. And I said to myself, well, that seems like a lot easier than writing books, and I think I can do this. And I had been editing a publication at the college, sort of a Black expressionist–type publication. I decided to sit down one Saturday and I jotted down or wrote out two or three columns, and then also clipped out some of my writings from the publication that I had contributed to in college, and sent it off to Ralph Otwell, managing editor of the *Chicago Sun-Times.* I didn't hear from him for a while and then I called him and got an appointment with him and found that he'd liked my writing. I ended up getting a job as an editorial assistant and I was given a column in a supplement of the paper that went to high schools; it had a circulation of fifty thousand. I wrote a weekly column and got paid an extra fifty dollars above my editorial assistant salary to write it.

MG: What did you write about?

EC: The subjects were basically whatever was going on at the time. The whole Black consciousness movement was taking place. And there was also a lot of politics in Chicago, and so I sort of drew my material from that. I even became more attuned to reading the newspaper every day because now I had to come up with material. So I was reading the newspaper. I was reading all kinds of magazines.

MG: Obviously reading was by now an integral part of your life personally and the life you wanted professionally. As a teacher of both journalism and creative writing on the university level, I have found that my students don't read much at all. What are your ideas for getting young people more interested in reading?

EC: I think the way to get young people reading is to read to them from a very early age and then to encourage them to read on their own. I have a daughter who is now nine. We read to her every night and she reads to us as well.

MG: What was your major in college? How did you prepare academically for a career in journalism?

EC: I majored in Psychology. I had decided that I didn't need to major in Journalism. For one thing I had not decided I wanted to be a journalist. I knew I wanted to be a writer.

MG: What's the difference between the two?

EC: I think it's the difference between the short term and the long term in some sense. It's the difference between writing something that's for immediate consumption and writing something that's for consumption over a longer period of time. It's the difference between writing articles and writing books. And I had sort of gotten into my head that I wanted to be this writer person, and that journalism would be interesting to do because it was immediate and paid the bills. And I also knew that James Baldwin hadn't even gone to college.

MG: So you always saw yourself being a journalist and a writer.

EC: Yeah. And so I had this idea that I wanted to do it without going to journalism school. I had this idea that studying psychology would really teach me a lot about people, and that it was important for me to understand people if I was going to be a writer.

MG: You're exactly right.

EC: So I decided to study psychology and happily I was offered a chance to write this column, and did that until the summer break came. That would have been the summer break of my sophomore year. And I got called into the editor's office, a guy named Jim Hoge.

And he says, "Ellis, I've been reading your columns in the *Viewpoint for Schools* and I like them; what do you think of writing a column for the *Chicago Sun-Times*?" I told him that's what I wanted to do all the time. He said, "Well, starting Monday you have an op-ed column in the *Chicago Sun-Times*." I said wonderful and that's how that got started.

So for my last two years in college I wrote my column once a week for the newspaper.

MG: What was the reaction of your family and friends to your writing a column for one of the country's major newspapers at the age of nineteen? That was a pretty big deal.

EC: You're right, it was a big deal because initially when I started writing, I think my parents just thought it was strange. But now all of a sudden my picture is in the newspaper. I'm appearing on television. The neighbors are calling up and saying, I saw Ellis. So it registered as something that was respectable and a good thing. My mother was very proud. She would clip my columns and keep them. So it went from we don't know what this kid is up to, to this is really cool. I did those two jobs, so it was a strange sort of college life. I really was not paying a whole lot of attention to college at that time. The staff at the newspaper were people twice my age.

So it was kind of an unusual college existence. I went through two years like that. Then when I graduated, I just got absorbed full time with the *Sun-Times*, and I came on board as a columnist/reporter.

MG: Clearly for you as a writer, reading and writing were the foundation for your professional life, but how do you argue for their broader importance?

EC: It's so fundamental to understanding the world. It's so fundamental to understanding different people and things you don't experience directly. I mean, one of the big ideas in my head when I began writing when I was sixteen or seventeen was the sense that there were these issues in my community that people outside of my community didn't understand that needed to be communicated. And there were these problems that other folks didn't see. There were these voices that weren't being heard. I had that sense that I could communicate to a larger community some vitally important things that were taking place in my community. As a journalist, I have traveled through most of the United States, and also through much of Europe, Africa, Latin America, and elsewhere. I don't think I have ever gone anywhere without reading about it first. So reading always helped to shape my impressions of the world. My life and my reading and writing are inseparable. Reading has not so much changed my life as shaped it.

MG: You've written books. You've got your column. What are the stories, when you think back over your career as a writer, as a journalist, that most changed or enlarged you, and why did they do that, and how did they do that?

EC: There are two different things that I think of immediately. I've spent quite a bit of time in South Africa, and particularly in the beginning of '96 when the Truth and Reconciliation Commission was set up. I spent a lot of time going back and forth to Brazil and a lot of time going back and forth to South Africa. I was going there for *Newsweek,* and for a book I was doing, and part of it was because I was involved in a task force that was funded by the Ford Foundation looking at race relations in different societies. In some ways the series of stories and writings that came out of that was very important to me. The way that people looked at race in South Africa was very different from the way we looked at it in America, and the way they looked at it in Brazil was very different still. It was eye-opening to sort of see the racial dynamics in various societies.

But the book that without question has had the most impact, based on what I hear back from people, is *The Rage of a Privileged Class.*

MG: I loved that book. It was so honest, and shattered so many myths.

EC: Thank you. To this day people will come up to me with a tattered copy and say, this book changed my life. Often people who are working in corporate settings tell me this book made me realize I wasn't crazy or that I wasn't alone. It's had just a huge impact. In a similar way, though not as large, *Envy of the World,* the book I wrote about Black men, had impact. I get lots of letters from lots of Black men and also women and people who aren't Black, who say that book spoke to them. I spoke to a group of young people once, a group of Black and Latino teenagers in New York, and they had read the book in preparation for my talk. One young man told me, "I never met an author before, and I've never read a Black book." He was just very impressed with that.

The other thing I think, and I'm going back, way, way, back, and this is just being young and not knowing much of anything, I covered my first presidential race, which was Carter. So that would have been when I was twenty-three I guess.

MG: And you were still with—

EC: The *Chicago Sun-Times.* It was my first big national

assignment, and all of a sudden I'm traveling on planes, talking with presidential candidates, and going with the Secret Service, and just experiencing all of that. For a, what, twenty-three-year-old kid who was from the slums of Chicago to watch that and to be close to that, was a place that I never imagined existed when I was a kid, much less that I would be close to.

MG: So writing is a passport into the world.

EC: Yeah. To go from a kid whose world was a very narrow world—at least in terms of what I had actually experienced and actually seen, a world where there wasn't a whole lot of diversity in terms of income, in terms of ethnicity, where the default position on opportunity was essentially there wasn't any—to this world where you have these young people who literally believe they can run the world, was incredible. So all of a sudden I'm associating with these people who literally thought it was their job to run the world. That was eye-opening for me because I just had not had that view of people around my own age who had those kinds of aspirations before.

MG: But even though you may not have grown up in the neighborhood or in an environment where it would be easily thought that you would grow up and run the world, clearly from a very early age you had a sense that you had a right to have input into the world through using language.

EC: Absolutely. Absolutely. I always had the sense that I could affect the way people felt about things, that I could inform the way people looked at things. The difference I guess between that and being around people who are trying to run the White House is the difference between influence and power. And that was my introduction to people who actually realistically aspired to power.

MG: Your radio project is called "Against the Odds." Why? What is it about that narrative that draws you?

EC: Probably a lot of it's personal. When I first began writing for the *Sun-Times* and my work began to get a little attention in Chicago, I remember getting this letter from somebody who I went to grade school with who was in prison. He wrote me not to ask me for anything. He wrote just to remind me that we had been in fourth grade together. I don't know what he was in prison for. Part of what he wrote was that I'm so happy that somebody got out; those were the words that he used. What's always engaged me is this whole question of how one person overcomes a set of challenging life experiences and another fails to. What are the things that happen along the way? And that's related to me and my experience in the projects and seeing myself and some other guys do very well and a whole lot of people not do well at all. It's a large part of the kind of journalism that I've done. I've focused on large communities and, often internationally, sometimes domestically, on what happens with people within that framework of choices and options.

So when we were explaining themes for this documentary series, that's one that resonated strongly and that I felt could allow us to look into communities and places that don't normally find a place in the mainstream media. We wanted to do it in a way that would not turn people off and would not have people say, well, I don't want to be depressed about reading about people who are impoverished and in despair.

MG: Who are a couple of the most fascinating people that you've met in your journalist career?

EC: Without a doubt, Nelson Mandela would be among them, and maybe Xanana Gusmão, who was the president of East Timor. They both underwent long periods of personal struggle in the transition of their countries. Mandela is fascinating because of the amount of time he was on Robben Island and then emerged from that to be the kind of person he is. But in addition to his story, there's being in his presence, as I've been fortunate enough to be a couple of times for a long period of time. He's just an extraordinary individual, and he's funny as well. And very much deferential, but with an aura that demands nicely that you defer to it because it's just powerful. And Gusmão has some of those same traits. He has a similar personality in some respects and also endured captivity for many years.

MG: What did they bring out of captivity?

EC: I think in both cases what they brought out of it was this awareness that there was nothing to be gained by lingering in bitterness. There's nothing to be gained by trying to force a retribution; that instead they had to come out with a spirit that could embrace humanity.

MG: And there is power in that.

ELLIS COSE RECOMMENDS

Invisible Man by Ralph Ellison

The Fire Next Time by James Baldwin

Crime and Punishment by Fydor Dostoyevsky

FAITH ADIELE *is a global literary explorer. In her books and essays she has mined the complexities and richness of her heritage (her mother is Nordic American, and her father was an Igbo from Nigeria) for narratives that speak a universal language. Her first book,* MEETING FAITH: THE FOREST JOURNALS OF A BLACK BUDDHIST NUN, *won the PEN Beyond Margins Award for Best Memoir.*

Separated from her father for many years, after he left the United States to return to Nigeria, Faith was raised in Sunnyside, Washington, where she was the only Black child in the area. Growing up on a small farm in a book-loving family, Faith's mother strove mightily to connect her to her identity as a person of color, mostly through books. She describes her parents' cross-cultural relationship as symbolic of the social and historical changes of the 1960s, the period during which they met at the University of Washington. Of her writing Faith has said, "My identity questions are quite public. They fuel my work. I use personal and family stories to illustrate the modern-day quest for nation and family."

In the essay "My African Sister," Faith explores the challenges of "coming home" to her father and her Igbo family during a visit to Nigeria; in "Black Men," she examines the history of mental depression among the men in her mother's family. Both essays poignantly link Faith's search for identity and place to the disconnections she has inherited.

Faith is also a popular speaker and contributor to magazines as diverse as ESSENCE, O, CREATIVE NONFICTION, *and* MS. *She is co-editor of the anthology* COMING OF AGE AROUND THE WORLD, *and received a BA in Southeast Asian Studies from Harvard and Radcliffe Colleges, an MA in Creative Writing from Lesley College, and MFAs from the University of Iowa in both Fiction and Nonfiction. Faith's story of her search for roots, family, and identity was featured as part of a PBS series* MY JOURNEY HOME.

MARITA GOLDEN: Because I've had the benefit of reading *Meeting Faith* and a number of your essays, I want to begin by talking about the essay you wrote about your mother.

FAITH ADIELE: She had always been a bookworm and read anything she could get her hands on. When she got to college, she really wanted to educate herself. I think first off she realized that she was racist, so she really wanted to kind of educate herself out of that. Then at a certain point she realized that she had internalized all this sexism, and so she wanted to educate herself out of that. And years later, when I came back from college and was talking about gender issues, gender roles, the people I'd met who had nontraditional sexual orientations, she was like, "Oh my God, I'm homophobic," and once again she was off to the bookstore!

MG: Did she inherit her love of reading from her family?

FA: Well, yes and no. Everybody in her family read a lot. There were twelve kids in my maternal grandfather's family. These were Swedish immigrants, and yet every birthday and every Christmas, each kid got a book of his or her own. That's twenty-four books bought by a father who was a laborer! My grandfather's father was working down on the docks. It wasn't high-level reading, but clearly reading was really, really valued, so I guess you could say that is a family value. My grandmother was also a voracious reader. Once a week when I was a kid, we'd leave the farm and go into town to the public library. This was something that they had done for years before I came along. When my mom was little, they would get nine books for her, one for every day of the week, and then two for the weekends. My grandmother would get cowboy books for my grandfather and my uncle, and English countrywomen horse books for herself and my great-aunt, and my mom was just steadily reading her way through everything. My mom told me a charming story about having read all the books in the children's section and trying to move to the adult books and being stopped by a librarian. They wouldn't let her check out adult books. My grandfather went down to the library and just scared the woman shitless. He told her in no uncertain terms, "I pay taxes, this is my daughter; when you see her, get out of the way; she's going to read any damn book she wants to."

MG: Did all that reading make your mother perhaps more open to the idea of being involved with your father? That was pretty bold, a young, small-town White girl, who had never really been exposed to people of different races or cultures, falling for a Nigerian.

FA: I think the reading played a part, but I think it also came from her family upbringing. Her family was politically radical and aware of class issues. Mom said she was always taught that all men are created equal, but poor people get into heaven faster.

MG: What were the books that you treasured and loved as a child?

FA: I loved mythology, particularly international mythology. My mom was very conscious about finding books that had brown kids in them, so she would go on these big excursions to Seattle and buy every book that had a brown face on it. It was a big deal. She would take the bus over to Seattle, two hundred miles away, and stock up on culture and toys, anything that was international and of color. For a long time, I guess because I was an only child and also the only person of color in my family, those books kept me company when I was trying to figure out my African identity. I don't think I had a sense of a Black identity at that point, but I knew part of me was African. I was much more of a bookworm than my peers and I wasn't terribly popular, or into sports, but books made me feel like I could read my way into those experiences and worlds that seemed off-limits to me.

MG: So seeing Black characters in books was obviously very important to you?

FA: Yes, it was books that taught me that Blacks could be powerful princesses and abolitionists and civil rights leaders and scientists. As a child I was obsessed with the Amistad Rebellion and the Haitian Revolution. I wanted to become a warrior, someone who fought for the rights of her people. For me the big breakthrough was reading about Igbo characters, first in Chinua Achebe and then in Buchi Emecheta. But I think I read these characters more as missing family members than as reflections of myself.

MG: How would your life have been different if you were not a reader?

Yes, it was books that taught me that Blacks could be powerful princesses and abolitionists and civil rights leaders and scientists.

FA: I don't know that I would have traveled if I hadn't read, would have known there was an entire world outside of the godforsaken small town where I was raised. Or known that I could be a writer.

MG: You teach graduate writing students. Does the decline in reading show up in your classes?

FA: Yes.

MG: How?

FA: Yes. My students don't read, and I teach people who are Writing majors, so it's just incredible. They read blogs. They read things I don't understand. I feel so old all of a sudden because they read and interact with the word in a completely different way than I do. And then every so often you get this old-fashioned kind of student who just loves books and will bring you things to read and scribble over his or her books, and it's just amazing.

MG: What do you think your students are losing because they read in this new way?

FA: One of the results of the lack of reading is that many of my writing students can't recognize when they are writing in clichés. They're not well educated enough to know.

MG: To know that what they've written has been written about eight million times before.

FA: Yes. I also find that they're not willing to engage in difficult texts and don't see the reward in effort that doesn't offer immediate satisfaction or understanding. So you have to teach them to have the patience to really engage and be challenged by a text. But once they have cracked a coded or a complicated text, they're really excited about it.

MG: Now as a biracial child, as a child of this mixed culture, what you said earlier seemed to imply that books in a sense saved you. What did books save you from?

FA: I guess from paying too much attention to the social dynamics of my town.

MG: Which were?

FA: It was very White, Republican, Born Again Christian, superficial, monied.

MG: So books gave you an alternative vision.

FA: Yes, exactly.

MG: Give me the names of one or two books from your childhood that you loved.

FA: Apparently I loved this book about two Haitian twins called *Marassa and Midnight*. They were originally Igbo, so we had the tribal thing, and they were twins, which is a recurring theme in my family story. I loved that book. Read it all the time. I even slept with it.

MG: Are there any books that you regularly reread?

FA: Yes. The first creative nonfiction book, the first book that told me I wanted to write creative nonfiction, was Michael Ondaatje's *Running in the Family*, so I read that a lot.

MG: Why?

FA: It's doing so many different things, and I was amazed that nonfiction could do that. He has poems in there, photographs, explorer's journals of encountering Sri Lanka, and family oral history. I'm not interested in a linear narrative, and it moves in a cyclical way. He creates a different type of discourse, and I thought, oh my god, nonfiction can do this? This is the genre I want to be writing! Prior to that, I had been a "thick novel" girl. I loved García Márquez's *Autumn of the Patriarch*, and I reread that. I loved *Crime and Punishment, Song of Solomon, No Longer at Ease.* Those are the books I always revisit.

MG: What is it about those texts that makes them an integral part of your intellectual life?

FA: Well with Morrison I loved *Song of Solomon* for so many reasons, for its craft, for Morrison's writing philosophy, that it referenced the myth of the Flying Igbos—the last boatload of slaves who took one look at the New World, shook their heads, and refused. Some say they walked back over the ocean to Africa, some say they drowned; but the important thing is that they refused/transcended. And they were from my tribe.

MG: Did *Song of Solomon* affect you as a writer?

FA: Morrison was my first literary mother. She says there is no reason that art and politics can't go hand in hand, that something can't be politically important and yet incredibly gorgeous. She shows our intimate connection to history.

MG: You cited *No Longer at Ease* by Chinua Achebe. That book must have had a special meaning for you because of your heritage.

FA: In the absence of my real father, Achebe, who actually went to school with my father, and is an old family friend, became my literary father and my cultural guide.

MG: Is there a book you think everyone should read?

FA: *A Small Place* by Jamaica Kincaid, to learn how to be better travelers and world citizens and to see that it's okay to be angry.

MG: What is it about nonfiction that has spoken to you so much more than fiction?

FA: It's having to create a metaphor out of facts. I love the puzzle in that and the challenge. It's like having to write a sestina, any kind of strong, dictated form. It's got to end with these words, and have this long stanza—stuff like that. You have to create something that's meaningful out of it and it's not just an exercise. To me, nonfiction gives you the same sort of limitations. You have these facts, but then you have to create art out of it with language and metaphor. I think it's stunning because I'm fascinated by the truth, and then I'm also fascinated by how fallible memory is. I love how I remember things and how I misremember things, and then how when your memory comes in contact with somebody else, it changes. I just love the process of memoir. It's not really true, but it's a truth. So I'm fascinated by that whole project and having to create metaphor and sense out of all this real detail. I just love the challenge.

MG: What nonfiction books would you suggest as indispensible for someone writing a memoir or autobiography?

FA: Patrica Hampl's *I Could Tell You Stories*. It's not a memoir; it's essays on the political importance of memoir and memory. I think it's brilliant. I have to say at this point that your book, *Migrations of the Heart,* and Maya Angelou's *All God's Children Need Traveling Shoes* were like my Bibles. I read them over and over and over again before I went to Nigeria.

MG: Thank you. Well, a big part of the story you have been telling in your writing is the story of being a person who is biracial. What is the story that being biracial gives you to tell the world?

FA: It gives you the ability to be a bridge or translate or see different worlds from the inside that our society has not really allowed people to see. Because this country is built on the distinction between the races, White and Black, and because also our Western thinking is so binary and dichotomous that we don't really have a language like they do in the East to talk about the middle path. There's really nothing in between. And so I think that politically and metaphorically, the biracial person has been a source of anxiety, and once we get over the anxiety, it's really the key to healing the country or being able to see these two things that have not been allowed to see each other. I think it's so rich. Beyond racial politics, just the way we wrap our mind around concepts I think has really been poisoned or limited by that kind of Western approach, the idea that things are good or bad, black or white, this or that.

MG: What's the pain in being biracial?

FA: Never being accepted. Not having a place that's entirely one's home, I guess, or being suspect, being a source of anxiety so people project things onto you.

MG: What was the genesis of your first book, *Meeting Faith*?

FA: Flunking out of Harvard! College was such a disappointment—the fact that it wasn't the intellectual Mecca I'd been seeking and few were interested in using our education to better the world, constantly being told I was only there because of Affirmative Action, constantly being told to choose between racial or gender concerns, the extreme segregation of Boston and the culture shock in moving from the rural Northwest to the urban Northeast. I completely imploded. I flunked my classes and had a breakdown. So I had to leave for a year.

Somehow I knew that returning to Thailand, where I'd spent a year as a high school exchange student, would be safe, that the East would provide a break from Western black/white thinking.

Originally I was looking for a fieldwork project to redeem my intellect, and I thought that studying Buddhist nuns, who were dismissed by Thai society and treated rather poorly by monks, would be perfect. All the nuns I'd met were kind of joyful and wise. Clearly, they had transcended their surroundings. Then, before I knew it, I'd shaved my head and eyebrows, put on the white robes of a Buddhist nun, and moved into the forest. Clearly I was seeking something beyond academic redemption. Only later did I discover that I'd chosen a temple in the Forest Tradition, an ascetic sect that takes a vow of silence, eats one meal a day, and spends nineteen hours a day in mindfulness. Oops! To keep me from going insane, the head nun gave me a journal. Years later, when I first had the idea for the book, it was just going to be journal entries. I transcribed the notes in my journal when I first got to graduate school and showed it to an agent. She said, "Oh, you're going to have to rewrite this whole thing as a memoir." I was really upset, and I said, "I can't rewrite this whole thing!" And she said, "It's all over the place. There might be scenes, but they're not developed. There's no distance reflecting on what you've learned. We're just in the middle of this, and we don't know how you got there." That seemed like such a huge project, but eventually I realized that she was right and that I needed to understand why I wanted to tell this story and what the story was really about. I figured early on that it's really not about Buddhism or even about spirituality, but it's a kind of coming-of-age story.

MG: The coming-of-age story is so universal and so beloved and is in many ways the foundation for so much literature, and that brings me to the question of why is reading important?

FA: I think it's one of the few ways you can learn empathy, you can really learn about people and enter into a new world, enter into something outside of yourself. I learn the most when I've been challenged, where I've had the rug pulled out from underneath me, and I've been smack up against my own limitations, and I've had to proceed on faith. That's when I've really learned the most. That happens a lot in travel, but it happens in reading, too.

MG: I think it happens in reading because a book is a journey. A good book is not stagnant. Why is writing important?

FA: Well, for me it's about entering the conversation and having an opportunity to find a perspective that may not have been represented yet. And one of the reasons I love memoirs so much is that it's a form that upends the traditional power structure of who gets to write history and whose voices get to be heard. Patricia Hampl says in her essays that it's politically important for us to create a narrative of who we are as individuals and who we are nationally, and if we don't, someone else will do it for us.

MG: What do you enjoy about teaching writing?

FA: Getting students excited about ideas and the world and relating to it through writing. Initially I didn't want to teach because both my parents were teachers, and I was doing community work. I was lured into teaching and told that the work I was doing training young people to be activists could happen in the classroom. What activates me as a teacher are questions like, What is it that you feel passionately about? What do you want to engage in? And I've also found that teaching is a way to help students connect their lives and identities to the larger culture. I just love opening their eyes and getting them really excited about this process. One of the joys of nonfiction is that everybody has a story in them. They may not have the imagination for a fictional story, but I feel that everybody has an interesting nonfiction story, and if I can give them the tools, they can actually write that story. And that's empowering for them. It's transformative, it's exciting, and so I love being part of that.

FAITH ADIELE RECOMMENDS

A Small Place by Jamaica Kincaid

Song of Solomon by Toni Morrison

Crime and Punishment by Fyodor Dostoyevsky

No Longer at Ease by Chinua Achebe

I Could Tell You Stories by Patricia Hampl

*We Wish to Inform You That Tomorrow We Will Be Killed
     Along With Our Families* by Philip Gourevitch

The Autumn of the Patriarch by Gabriel García Márquez

EDWARD P. JONES

is considered by many to be the literary laureate of Washington, D.C.'s African-American community. His short stories reveal the poetry and grandeur woven into the seemingly ordinary lives of generations of Black migrants to the city. In prose that is hyp notically beautiful in its sophisticated simplicity, Jones dramatizes life as it has been and is lived in what is often called "the other Washington." In the short story collections LOST IN THE CITY *and* ALL AUNT HAGAR'S CHILDREN, *the resilience of the lives of ordinary Black "folk" far from the reach of the power centers activates catharsis and revelation.*

Edward P. Jones experienced the kind of literary success with the publication of his second book, and first novel, THE KNOWN WORLD, *that is the stuff of most writers' fantasies. The novel, a breathtakingly beautiful meditation on slavery, race, history, and the bondage that both love and hate can become, was published to wide-spread critical acclaim. The book received the 2004 Pulitzer Prize for Fiction, the National Book Critics Circle Award, was a finalist for the National Book Award, won the International IMPAC Dublin Literary Award, and the Lannan Literary Award. And Jones received a MacArthur "Genius" Grant.*

In the course of our conversation about his beginnings as a reader and writer, Jones praised his mother as an important and crucial source of his strength and confidence. Although his mother could not read, she recognized the importance that books held for her studious son. In more ways than most could imagine, Jones says his mother made him a writer.

The dedication in ALL AUNT HAGAR'S CHILDREN *is an eloquent testimony to the stories Jones has laid claim to and the manner in which those stories reflect his family's life. The dedication reads in part "... to the multitudes who came up out of the South for something better, something different, and again, to the memory of my mother, Jeanette S. M. Jones, who came as well and found far less than even the little she dared hope for."*

MARITA GOLDEN: Was the environment in your home as a child one that encouraged reading?

EDWARD P. JONES: My mother had a Bible, but she couldn't read or write. So if she needed anything, I would read to her.

MG: What did you read as a child?

EJ: DC Comics had a big variety of characters, everyone from Superman to Batman to Flash, Green Lantern, and Aqua Man. But around '61 or so, Marvel comics came out, and I took a liking to those characters, especially Spiderman, who was trying to help his aunt out with the rent. And the Marvel people had vulnerabilities it seemed to me. The DC Comics people were, once I began to read the Marvel people, on the one-dimensional side.

MG: I grew up in D.C. as well, around the same time, and one of my great joys was going to the library after school. Did you spend time in the public library?

EJ: Yes, after school. My sister and a few of our friends, we would go about seven or eight blocks down K and New York Avenue to the library. It was a nice, inviting place. Many of the books there when you walked in on the left were the books that had drawings in them, illustrations. I never bothered in those years to go to the books without pictures. For some reason, I needed to see whoever it was that I was reading about. So you would get the troll under the bridge. For some reason, that sort of supplemented what I was reading.

Then in 1964, the same year they passed the Civil Rights Bill, I was in South Boston, Virginia. My sister and I were with my aunt and her kids, and I ran out of funny books.

And my cousin's husband, he worked, but he often went to the junkyard and salvaged stuff, and he would salvage a lot of books. And one of the things he found was a regular book without pictures, and it was a British mystery. That was the first book I think I ever read that didn't have any pictures. I was thirteen and there were words in it that I wasn't really sure about, like the word "bungalow," but over a few pages you learn a bungalow is some sort of house. So whenever I came across the word "bungalow," that's what I would see.

Then the following summer I was with another aunt in Brooklyn, New York. I was still reading funny books in my spare time, but she had the second and third books that I ever read without pictures, one was *His Eye Is on the Sparrow*, an autobiography by Ethel Waters, and the other was *Native Son* by Richard Wright. By now, I was realizing you could read a book and create your pictures just based on what the author was saying.

MG: How did those books affect you?

EJ: Well, with *Native Son*, from the first line of it, the family is battling this rat. So right away, I'm in a situation in the book that I know very well. I know what these people are going through, and I had never come across Black people in a book. Of course, there were none of them in the comic books that I read, and at that point, I had read hundreds and hundreds. But I think just what fascinated me is that these people lived in Chicago. I had never seen anyplace but Brooklyn, and South Boston, Virginia, and North Carolina. I had never seen Chicago, but I could see it based on what Wright was saying, and there were Black people. It was as if they were living upstairs or downstairs from where I was living. And the same thing with Ethel Waters. Even though it was a rural environment where she grew up, the things she talked about, the foods and everything, the kind of life she lived, it was all very familiar.

When you see that the world you know can be put into words, it opens a door in your mind.

When I was in the tenth grade, I had a teacher named Charlotte Crawford. She was a thin woman, a Black woman with glasses, and she was in a masters degree program at Howard University. The first book she gave us was a paperback copy of *Black Boy*. Somewhere along the line I just never went back; I never turned back to funny books.

MG: So seeing yourself in the books, what did that mean to you about what books could be or what books could do? How did it shift you? Was it important that you were seeing Black people in books?

EJ: Yes, although Wright's picture was not on the back of *Black Boy; Go Tell It on the Mountain* did have James Baldwin's face on the back, a very tiny picture. There was a photo of Ellison on the back of *Invisible Man*. While reading the book I'd be grabbed by something on the page, and I would turn to that photograph and say, "You wrote that." I liked reading Wright and Baldwin because they were living *my* life. I was fascinated that people could put *that* life into words. When you see that the world you know can be put into words, it opens a door in your mind.

MG: How important was it for you as a reader, that your mother couldn't read and you, apparently, were reading quite actively?

EJ: I think she was glad that I was reading because it meant that I wasn't getting into trouble. I was always a good student, so she had nothing to worry about on that score. I remember when I was in high school, one of her jobs was cleaning up the restaurant where she worked, peeling potatoes, washing dishes, cleaning up the bathrooms. One day, she found a book. She didn't know what it was. She just knew it was a nice book. It wasn't a pornographic book, but on the bottom of the cover, there was the back of a naked woman, and there was a man embracing the woman. I don't remember what the book was about, but I think that she figured I might find it interesting. It never occurred to her that it might be something untoward, and it really wasn't. It was just a provocative cover to sell the book.

MG: But she was aware of your interest in reading and, in a sense, was nurturing it.

EJ: I think she thought that it was helping me. She couldn't have known how it was helping me, but she was glad I was reading. After a while, I didn't go outside anymore. My whole day was just going to school, and coming back home, and reading, and watching TV. It was a very simple life. We moved so much that I just didn't have it in me to make friends anymore. The kind of life that I had as a result of just staying home, and being bookish, and going off to college, that kind of life might not have been available to me if I'd been more outgoing.

MG: So in a way, would it be fair to say that books saved you?

EJ: They were the foundation of whatever it is I became.

MG: What journey were the books taking you on?

EJ: I just knew that I would pick up, for example, *Studs Lonegan*, which is three hundred, or four hundred pages, and my first thought wasn't, geez, this is too long for me to read, but it was, what is this guy going to tell me? What am I going to learn? Somewhere along the way I discovered Ann Petry's *The Street*, and Anne Moody's *Coming of Age in Mississippi*. I think what captured me most in those first years before I started venturing out in terms of what I read, were primarily stories about Black and White southern people; all I knew was the South, my mother and everybody else. But then you sort of branch out so that by the time I was a sophomore, junior, senior in high school, I had been reading a lot more; for example, I read Capote's *In Cold Blood*.

MG: Why is reading important?

EJ: Well, for me, I don't think I would have done as well in college if I had gone there afraid to pick up a book. But reading was second nature. You pick up a book, not with any sort of fear, but again, with the question, What am I going to learn? Where am I going to be taken? And so I think that the very fact that reading was important for me meant that I could go through the courses that I had in college and do just as well as these people who had had private-school educations. At that time, I think that the education I got at Cardozo Senior High allowed me to do very well in college, and I got a good one because I did read.

MG: Was there any element of escape for you?

EJ: I think it was just you pick up a book and you open a door and step into another place.

MG: Do you think reading has particular value for African Americans, people of color?

EJ: I remember when I was growing up, we didn't really read newspapers, but you knew who Ralph Bunche, the first African-American Nobel Peace Prize winner, was. But nowadays, kids if they ever pick up a newspaper, the first thing they go to is the Sports section. When I was growing up, you could hear people saying they wanted to be a policeman, a doctor and everything else, maybe now and again being some sort of ball player, maybe now and again being a singer. But people had ambitions, and it was harder going than it is now, I think. But it was never narrow to the point of only wanting to bounce a ball for a living or get an album done. They didn't have an idea of how much work went into being a doctor, but they thought that, yeah, I can attain that.

MG: I think that what you're talking about is a kind of cultural literacy that was very broad.

EJ: Things seeped down because of reading.

MG: I've been amazed to talk to young Black high school students who tell me in all honesty that many of their fellow students only think in terms of basketball or singing as a profession, and that it doesn't matter that there's been Black astronauts. It doesn't matter that there's a world-famous surgeon like Ben Carson because since those people don't live next door to them, they don't have an impact. But what you seem to be saying is that if these students read books about such people, those people could have an impact whether they lived in their neighborhoods or not. The story of their lives is in books.

EJ: Exactly. You wouldn't know until you read his book that Ben Carson did not start out with parents as doctors. You would not know that unless you read the story of his life. If you don't read, you might not learn that that kind of life is your right, and all you have to do is grab it. We learned that in the books, and even those of us who didn't read had a sense that with a lot of hard work that was possible.

MG: Books can help you understand that through the journeys that the heroes and the heroines made, and also I think just through your commitment to read about them.

EJ: And not being frightened of two hundred pages. I have to do this preface for a book that compiles a series of articles the *Washington Post* did on Black men. At one end, there's this guy who's in his twenties with a kid, and he doesn't live with the mother or the kid, and he considers himself a good father by doing the very basics. There's a guy in and out of prison and he is complaining now that he can't get a job. Then there are these men in Prince Georges County in their sixties, retired, who know that there's racism out there, but who came from a generation where the first enemy on the road to where you want to get to is yourself, and if you over- come yourself, then you have more strength to confront the larger enemy out there.

It's obvious in the articles that those kind of people are rare now. They're dying out. They knew that it's going to be hard, but they hadn't crippled themselves by breaking the law all along the way. One of the things I realized, I suppose, is that if I didn't have reading and if I wasn't the kind of person who didn't want to really break my mother's heart, if I had come home from school and not been a reader, then I would have been out in the street, and I don't know what I would have found. Reading was very, very important.

MG: What were some of your other favorite books around the time you were in high school?

EJ: *Uncle Tom's Children* by Richard Wright, because of the suffering and dying and it being set in Mississippi. The stories of southern writers always seemed very familiar to me. I liked *The Chosen* by Chaim Potok because it was about a friendship between two boys.

MG: Is there any book you would say that everyone ought to read?

EJ: The Bible, not because of any religious ideas, but because you can be entertained and moved forever by the stories it contains.

MG: How has writing shaped and expanded your life?

EJ: For a long time writing wasn't really all that important to me, not as much as it should have been. I was never one to get up every day and do it. From '83 on until '88, '89, I would just do it every now and again. Then on this day job that I had, there were two guys there who died, and they had wanted to be writers. I think that I felt rather guilty about the fact that a lot of people had said that I could write and I wasn't doing it, and these guys who wanted to do it were no longer around. So I started working on *Lost in the City.* I think what happens with the writing is that, you can get up depressed or with a heavy heart, and if you can put in two or three good pages and be happy by noon with those pages, then there's a kind of chemical transformation.

MG: So you're talking about the transformational power of writing.

EJ: Yeah. And I think, we're born with these things that can help us get over difficulties, but a lot of us don't realize it. We're born, some of us, with this ability to play the violin, but we never know it, to paint pictures, to write, but we never discover we can do that. We go through life in a down state, not that even if we knew that we could play the violin, not that that would save us from a lot of things. But it would be one thing that we could grab onto and hold.

I lived in this apartment in Arlington from '83 until 2004, twenty-one years. After *Lost in the City* came out, I had been thinking up this thing that became a novel, *The Known World.* But I hadn't really sat down and done any writing. In '99, these new people bought the apartment building, and they didn't make the people above me on the tenth floor put down carpeting and they were loud and noisy and that really had an effect on me. I had already suffered a bout of depression and been on and off medicine.

It was one of the worst times ever in my life. There are about four or five things I can point to in life along this line, and the first one is the death of my mother, and this four-and-a-half-year period from '99 to 2004 with these people above me was another. I suffered through all of that, and at times I would take this medicine. For all those years, the book *The Known World* was gelling in my head. Then I lost the day job that I had for nineteen years. I wondered how was I going to get a job? But rather than saying, you have no job, what are you going to do now, I had a plan for the novel because I had been working on it for ten years in my head. And the writing of it said you can put aside the misery for now. The job is to do five pages a day. These people that were in the novel, they carried me through. And over time, as more and more of the book came out on the computer, the pain of it all was banished. I was writing the book based on all the books I have ever read, knowing what was good and what was not good. Knowing that you can't be stereotypical, that every character you come up with, whether Black or White, has to be given his or her due. Even the worst criminal in the novel, there was a moment when this person was a good person perhaps, whether it was when they were one or two years old. Your job with the worst person in the novel is to find out when that day was. When you write, you want to go down a road that no other writer has gone down.

MG: I think that the act of writing isn't just always sitting down in front of the computer.

EJ: Well, before, I would have said it was the physical thing, but now I give credit to the process of thinking it out. That's writing as well. Years ago, I would not have said what goes on in the head is part of it. So, yeah, thinking it out saved me a great deal because it meant that the day after I lost my job, I could get up and I knew that I was going to go on.

MG: Go on with your life?

EJ: And with the writing. At that time, my life was the writing. If I hadn't had the writing, I don't know what would have happened. That's why I say people need to go out and discover this thing that some of us are born with.

MG: I know that you talk frequently about your work before audiences of young people in high school and college. What do you say specifically to African-American youth about the impact of reading and writing?

EJ: I tell them that reading and writing are the foundation for becoming a better person and having a better life. What I couldn't get from my mother I got from books and writing. Reading lets you know you are not alone in the world.

MG: Who would you say is your writing hero? I don't mean another writer, but a person or persons who gave you a sense that you could write, you should write, and maybe that the world was going to be incomplete without your stories?

EJ: It might be several people. The professor I had during my second year at Holy Cross in my very first creative writing course. He wasn't really the first person to say that what I was doing was fine, but I think it was the first time that I really did stories. I think when Charlotte Crawford, my teacher at Cardozo, gave me a copy of *Black Boy*, that was really important.

In the three books that I've done, in every case, in the dedication, I cite her. The first time it was just Charlotte Crawford's name alone, and in the second and third books, it's her name after other people's names. I dedicate my books also to my mother. For as long as there are libraries with the books that I've written, their names will be remembered there.

EDWARD P. JONES RECOMMENDS

The Bible

Native Son by Richard Wright

The Chosen by Chaim Potok

Go Tell It on the Mountain by James Baldwin

Invisible Man by Ralph Ellison

EDWIDGE DANTICAT

"What I fear most is the loss of loved ones. Maybe this book was a rage against it." That is Edwidge Danticat on her family memoir, BROTHER, I'M DYING. *The book, which won the National Book Award for Nonfiction, is a wrenching account of the deaths of her father and uncle and the birth of her first child; loss, gain, and renewal are all woven together in the haunting, lyrical voice Danticat's readers have come to know and love.*

When Danticat was two, her father fled Haiti to escape the murderous Tonton Macoutes, and her mother joined him in Brooklyn two years later. Danticat and her brother were cared for by an uncle, until they joined their parents in the United States nearly a decade later.

Political repression, exile, the stubborn endurance of family ties, and death are all themes activating this story, which surely was one of the hardest stories Edwidge Danticat has yet had to tell. Yet these are the issues she plumbs in all her work.

Since the publication of her debut novel, BREATH, EYES, MEMORY, *Danticat has expertly excavated the cultural history and the psychological wounds of her battered, sometimes broken but proud native country in the short story collections* KRIK? KRAK! *and* THE DEW BREAKER *and in the novel* THE FARMING OF BONES. *Danticat's stories have humanized people who are too often the objects of pity or scorn.*

Edwidge Danticat lives with her husband and daughters in Miami, where she writes and occasionally teaches. In our conversation she remembered the first stories she heard and loved that were part of the Haitian oral tradition. We talked about our shared passion for the novels of the great women Victorian writers, and how writing has provided someone who is in her own words "quite shy" with a way to speak boldly to the world.

MARITA GOLDEN: When you were living in Haiti as a young child, were you a writer?

EDWIDGE DANTICAT: I wasn't necessarily a writer then,

but I loved to listen to stories. My brothers and I had a lot of opportunities to hear stories because we didn't have a television until we were much older and even when we finally got one, it was not on all the time. We didn't have regular electricity, so at night I remember rushing through my homework so that I could hear stories, particularly the stories of Granmè Melina, the nearly hundred-year-old mother-in-law of my uncle.

MG: I remember her vividly from your memoir, *Brother, I'm Dying.*

ED: She was, in my opinion, the best storyteller in the whole neighborhood because a lot of the kids would come and listen to her tell her stories. So for me, like many writers, the seeds for my becoming a writer were planted in my listening to stories. And often the storytelling sessions involved the recycling of some of the same stories because there are certain patterns in most storytelling. In Granmè Melina's stories there was often someone clever and then there was someone more clever. There was an injustice that was done, then there was an injustice that was righted. This reminds me very much of a lot of southern American stories. I think we all have the same sources as children of the African diaspora. This very old woman who seemed so powerless in other places in her life—who was sick, who was poor—became very lively when she was telling a story. I remember sitting before her as a child thinking, oh, I'd like to do that. I'd like to tell stories too. But I was very shy. When I started reading books, the first book given to me by my uncle Joseph was a book called *Madeline* by Ludwig Bemelmans.

MG: I loved *Madeline.*

ED: I think there's something in that little girl to cling to. I've already introduced the book to my daughter, who is now three. We read it in both French and English and my daughter really loves it now. When I started reading *Madeline* I got a sense that, oh, there's another way you can tell stories. If you're shy, you can write stories down. I later came to think that of course, you lose something when you write a story down, but of course there is a lot you lose in the orality, too, because once the storyteller is gone, the stories may die with him or her.

MG: Right, but what you gain with a book is a larger audience. Clearly Grànmè Melina brought the community together. A lot was happening in that storytelling, it seemed to me, not just telling a story, but she was confirming community. She was confirming family relationships. She was confirming your relationship to people who you didn't even know existed. But as you say, when you write something down, maybe you lose that intimacy, but then you reach all these other thousands and thousands of readers, who become in a sense, part of your extended family.

ED: Yes, absolutely. In migration, the ground shifts under you; you don't have the same rules. You don't have the same structures in place. It's especially helpful when you're in migration to have had that transition from the oral to the written because the grandmother cannot always come with you. I'm glad that I had been told stories as well as being given stories to read in a book because then reading and writing seemed like a natural progression of that oral process.

MG: Clearly you were hungry to read books because your

appetite had been whetted by that strong oral tradition, and you had been introduced to an entrancing young female hero in *Madeline,* one that clearly got your imagination going. A storyteller from your native culture and a children's book writer from the West were your foundation; would that be a fair way to put it?

ED: Absolutely. And I also think that reading as a new twelve-year-old immigrant in America was a way for me to better understand my new environment. It was a way for me to process what was around me. When I got here, I felt like I'd understand everything once I'd read about it.

MG: Right. Besides *Madeline,* what did you read in Haiti?

ED: We read also French literature, which I remember because that reading was framed around school. We read excerpts from *Candide* by Voltaire. And then we read parts of Emile Zola and Alexandre Dumas père, who had a Haitian grandmother. But we were never taught any contemporary or older Haitian writers at that point. Now that's changed some. But we didn't read anybody local, and for most of my teachers, their idea of true literature was French literature. Even though we had been severed from the French colonial experience since we gained our independence from France in 1804, French literature was still taught to us as though everything that was beautiful, everything that was educated or quote, unquote, "civilized" was French. I grew up thinking that good literature was written by French dead men because those were the people we read. I started reading Haitian literature when I got to the United States because I was homesick for Haiti, and since I didn't speak English, that was all that I could read at the library. I remember my first trip to the Brooklyn Public Library; they had two shelves of Haitian books in the foreign book section, and I just went through them so quickly!

MG: So you had to come to the United States to delve into your Haitian literary heritage because those books were not made available to you in school or at home?

ED: That's right. And I'm not alone in that. I think that is true for a whole generation of people. Maybe if I had gone further in school in Haiti, eventually I would have been taught Haitian literature, but at the level that I was in primary school, we weren't taught any Haitian writers. Even the things we memorized, they were these French poems for children.

MG: Who are one or two of the Haitian writers that you discovered when you got here?

ED: One of them was Jacques Roumain. His most famous novel is called *Masters of the Dew*. In the 1940s, it was translated by Langston Hughes and Mercer Cook from French to English. Hughes had traveled to Haiti and he and Roumain became good friends. Jacques Roumain wrote many poems that he dedicated to Langston Hughes, and Roumain also wrote several poems about racism in America and lynching. The other writer is Marie Chauvet, one of our great novelists. Jacques Stephen Alexis, another one of our great writers, wrote a phenomenal book called *Compère Général Soleil* (*General Sun, My Brother*), which is in part about the 1937 massacre of Haitian cane workers in the Dominican Republic. This was a great inspiration for my own novel on the subject, *The Farming of Bones*.

MG: What was the impact of encountering Black characters in books for the first time?

ED: Reading African, African-American, and Caribbean writers, I became aware of the diaspora and its implications. Suddenly through books there was a place where I belonged when I went to Africa or the U.S.

MG: When did you begin writing your first stories?

ED: I started writing in high school. There was a newspaper in New York called *New Youth Connections* and all the writers were New York City kids from different high schools. I saw it in my high school one day and decided to write something for the paper. I sent them a piece about how we, as Haitians, celebrate Christmas. I was fourteen and really had just acquired English. I was doing it as an exercise to see if people would understand what I wrote. Then I sent that to the paper and they published it. Kids from the school—and I was very shy—people who just didn't even see me saw that article, and they were like, oh, you wrote this. And I think I sort of got the bug from that moment.

MG: How did your parents react?

ED: It's been the same throughout my publishing life. I've just always been so shy about showing them things because I felt like I could so easily be corrected by them, that I would get things wrong, and that they had the better version of our experience. So I didn't show them that. But when I did publish other things later on, they saw the things that I wrote and sometimes they were concerned, because my parents had both spent the majority of their lives under a dictatorship, so

I think to them, this idea of self-revelation was rather dangerous. I think it's good that I didn't show them a lot of my writing because what I imagine they would have said was, be careful. Or stop.

MG: And a writer can't do that.

ED: Exactly. I think maybe I had a sense of writerly self-preservation that kept me from showing them my writing. I wrote for that student paper throughout all the four years that I was in high school. And then the last thing I wrote for them was about my first day in the United States, about coming here and getting on the escalator at the airport, and having the sense that it was like traveling through time because it was all really, really new. That piece started me on writing *Breath, Eyes, Memory,* my first novel.

MG: As someone for whom migration and exile are important themes both in your life and in your writing, how have reading and writing shaped your place in the world?

ED: They have helped me put the world in context, they have allowed me to place myself in a continuum with the rest of the world.

MG: What did writing mean to you then and what does it mean to you now?

ED: It's funny because it means ultimately the same thing now as it did at the very beginning. I feel so much joy when I'm writing, and even if I'm writing the saddest thing, then I guess you can say I feel a sense of contentment. I get so much pleasure from it. I get a sense of escape. And there is the sense of starting a journey.

MG: You attended Barnard as an undergraduate and

Brown for your MFA in Creative Writing. How did those experiences affect you as a reader and as a writer?

ED: Very powerfully. While I was at Barnard, I knew I was there with the daughters of the American ruling class, so to speak, although there were a lot of girls like me, immigrant girls, poor girls too. I had taken Advanced Placement classes in high school, but I almost felt like I had somehow stumbled into being there. One of my favorite professors there was a brilliant African-American woman named Quandra Prettyman. She was an extraordinary professor. She was one of the first Black women to get African-American studies into Barnard. And I remember in one of her classes we were reading *Jane Eyre*, and I said, oh, I would have loved to have been Jane Eyre. And she said something like, my dear it might have been complicated for you to be Jane Eyre. Later she told me to read Jean Rhys's *Wide Sargasso Sea*, which I had not read before and suddenly I got it. That's the brilliance of an education like that and a professor like that. Even if you were behind in scholarship before you got there, you get to have these moments.

MG: *Jane Eyre* was one of my favorite books, too, by the way.

ED: I was still young enough to have so much unrequited love in my life that I could so identify with the romance and failure of romance in both Brontë's and Rhys's books. Coming from a colonial experience, the hard part of course is to read certain authors and to realize that either they had disdain for Black people or they just didn't realize they existed. That's why *Wide Sargasso Sea* is such an important book. Also because I was at Barnard, there was the fact that it was a women's college and there was a kind of transcendent affiliation we felt with those women writers. At Barnard, Zora Neale Hurston had been the first Black woman to graduate, and so the echoes of her footsteps were there.

MG: Would you name some contemporary Haitian writers that you think American readers should know about?

ED: Well, in Canada and maybe some American readers would know him, there's a wonderful Haitian writer, Dany Laferrière. His best known book is a book called *How to Make Love to a Negro Without Getting Tired*. It's a great title. He followed that book with a collection of great fact/fictional essays called *Why Must a Black Writer Write About Sex?*

MG: I'm sensing a theme here.

ED: The French version, if it were literally translated, it would be "the grenade in the hand of the young writer is not a grenade, but a pen." And he also has one called *Dining with the Dictator*. His latest book is called *I Am a Japanese Writer*, because his whole notion of writers and readers is very invested in this idea that all writers live in the land of their readers, so that we take on, at least in the imagination, the identity of the reader. So if you're being read in Japan, you're a Japanese writer.

MG: I love that idea.

ED: I think he's sort of one of our best-kept secrets in terms of writers. And he's hilarious. His work is funny, but it's also very serious at the same time. Now in Haiti there are several wonderful writers. Yanick Lahens, Ketly Mars, Evelyne and Rolph Trouillot, Gary Victor, Paulette Poujol—they are names I know American writers will know better one day.

We have great poets, too, and short story writers among them: Marilène Phipps, Rodney Saint-Éloi, James Noel, Patrick Sylvain, and Danielle Georges, Katia Ulysse. Some of these writers are featured in an anthology I edited called *The Butterfly's Way: Voices from the Haitian Dyaspora in the United States.*

MG: How was shifting from fiction to autobiography in *Brother, I'm Dying* different? I know clearly you were just so justifiably angry about what happened to your uncle—who was elderly and quite sick during his detention in the custody of U.S. immigration officials, and who died there—that I can see that you had to write the book. But talk about that process.

ED: When I envisioned myself as a writer, I always wanted to be the kind of writer who was going to try to work between the genres because for me it keeps things a lot more interesting. I did a short nonfiction book some years ago, a book called *After the Dance,* on carnival in Haiti. That was really my first foray into nonfiction. And I loved it. I loved the process of finding things, facts, histories, as opposed to having to make them up. I loved this other sense of unearthing, of discovery in that process. I loved finding a way to put the facts together, to sort them out and marry them in an interesting way. So when my uncle died in immigration custody because of negligence and frankly cruelty from the U.S. immigration service, I felt like I had to write this book. But I'm glad that I had the practice of that little nonfiction book on a happier subject, especially with the heightened emotions of the story of both my uncle and father's deaths, which I tell in *Brother, I'm Dying.* One of the biggest things I wrestled with in *Brother, I'm Dying* is how to tell a story like that, how you organize it, because it was also a story that involved my father who was dying of a terminal illness at the same time that my daughter was being born, at the same time that my uncle was dying in the way we've already talked about. You put all three things together, and have feelings of anger, happiness, and it could easily have been a big sort of mess that takes several years to sort out before you even think of writing about it.

Writing is our footmark in the world.

MG: We are in a moment right now where both acts, reading and writing, seem sometimes to be under siege, but they have meant a lot to you why?

ED: Reading is important—although we can so easily go into platitudes here—because it expands your mind, your life. It extends your world. It's traveling without a passport. I feel like there are people in my life I will never know as well as the people in the books that I've read. I believe that it's the duty of every truly free citizen to read, especially to read beyond your borders, to read and read extensively. Writing is our footmark in the world. We're still looking at cave writings of centuries ago and are asking, what were they saying? It's one of the most important gifts we leave the world. How we leave it evolves all the time, whether it'll be the book, whether it'll be some other way. Even oral people, people who didn't necessarily write, masters of the oral traditions, we pore over their words centuries later looking for ourselves. By speaking or writing words down we leave a big trace behind, a big trace of ourselves and our cultures.

MG: Obviously writing transported you beyond the world of your parents.

ED: It's been a ticket out and a ticket in simultaneously. I step outside of my own and my parents' experience in order to render it and yet I have to do it objectively. I'm on a quest every day I write, to find out who I am. I consider it a great privilege to be able to do this. I've had the luxury of living an examined life.

MG: We've talked about a lot of writers, but who are the one or two writers that absolutely expanded your sense of what it's possible for a writer to do? Who would you name?

ED: I would say Marie Chauvet, author of *Amour, Colère et Folie*. She wrote these novels that were very political and also very erotic and very personal about subjects ranging from colorism to oppression by the dictatorship. She also wrote *Love, Anger, Madness*. When the book was published, they were going to publish it in France, then her family was threatened by the regime in Haiti, and so she had to send a relative to France to buy up the stock, five thousand copies of the book, because otherwise they would have all been killed. I just love her magic as a writer. She wrote several books after that that were published after she died. She writes from the perspective that writing is a room of one's own, a country of one's own. And the struggle to write under those circumstances and still write something brilliant I think is extraordinary. So I find her extraordinary and inspiring as a writer, woman, and exiled person. She died in exile here in the United States in the 1970s. But when I look back at women writers, when you look back at the life of Zora Neale Hurston, you look back at these women's lives and really all the sacrifices they made for their art, and then you always have to wonder what lay buried inside them or how much more they could have flourished. And it really keeps you, . . . I think for me it's helped me very much to focus on how grateful we should be to be able to practice our art.

MG: What are some of the books you absolutely cherish and would recommend to others?

ED: *Song of Solomon* by Toni Morrison. I feel it is such an epic, so grand and it's a book I study and enjoy because it takes me so deep. *I Know Why the Caged Bird Sings* by Maya Angelou is the first book I read in English with a dictionary. The brutal honesty struck me as a revelation. *Their Eyes Were Watching God* by Zora Neale Hurston reminded me that when you read southern writers, there are so many common cultural threads joining the Black community wherever we are.

MG: What is your argument in favor of reading?

ED: Reading is a place where you can have a village and be an individual at the same time, and it's totally transformative. It changes who you are, and you can reach out to the larger world.

MG: What should young African Americans know about the importance of reading and writing?

ED: That books and writing are part of our history, that Black people fought and died for the right to do both, and that you can still be liberated by the books you read and the words you write.

EDWIDGE DANTICAT RECOMMENDS

Amour, Colère et Folie and *Love, Anger, Madness*
   by Marie Chauvet
Song of Solomon by Toni Morrison
Their Eyes Were Watching God by Zora Neale Hurston
I Know Why the Caged Bird Sings by Maya Angelou
How to Make Love to a Negro Without Getting Tired
   by Dany Laferriere

Part II

Reading for the Mind

> "*Every time I think I know who I am, when I write, I get to smash that.*"
>
> —Mat Johnson

IMAGINATION IS THAT JOYFULLY COMBUSTIBLE INTERAC-
tion between the unknown and the possible, the tangible and
our fantasies. Reading can be a great leap beyond what we
think we know into the realm of the surprising. The writers in
this section, inspired by the prowess and beauty of what they
read in books, turned to writing to unleash the *inevitable* in
themselves, and to step forth onto both a public and private
center stage.

Einstein said it best: "*Imagination is more important than
knowledge.*" Someone imagined the book; someone imagined

the Kindle, which provides new ways of experiencing books. Imagination precedes everything we do, believe, fear, hope, or commit to.

For these writers, the results of sustained reading and writing have been minds that are in a constant search mode for the unlikely and the unexpected, both in themselves and in the subjects that they bring to life in their work.

PEARL CLEAGE

Novelist, playwright, journalist, and essayist Pearl Cleage has been creating African-American women heroes and speaking uncomfortable truths for more than three decades. Her father, Rev. Albert Cleage, founded a Detroit-based bookstore and cultural center, The Shrine of the Black Madonna, which was a national gathering place for some of the most important artistic and intellectual voices of the Black Arts Movement. Detroit, Houston, and Atlanta are currently home to Shrine of the Black Madonna bookstores.

Growing up in a politically conscious and active family that emphasized Black Pride before it was "in," and coming of age in the sixties, profoundly influenced the work of this prolific and popular author.

A resident of Southwest Atlanta, where she lives with her husband, writer Zaron Burnett, Pearl Cleage has in her recent novels used that community as a metaphor for a continuing dramatic exploration of the problems and promise of contemporary African-American urban life. In her plays, from FLYIN' WEST, a drama about a group of Black women living in Kansas in the 1880s, to A SONG FOR CORETTA, a celebration of the life and legacy of Coretta Scott King, Cleage is dedicated to heralding the often unspoken, unhonored, difficult experiences of Black women. Whether the issue is spousal abuse as in her book MAD AT MILES or AIDS in WHAT LOOKS LIKE CRAZY ON AN ORDINARY DAY, Cleage's readers can count on her to "tell it like it is."

The author of six novels, including most recently TILL YOU HEAR FROM ME, Cleage won the 2007 NAACP Image Award for Fiction for her novel BABY BROTHER'S BLUES. We talked over lunch in a restaurant in one of the hotels lining Atlanta's famous Peachtree Street.

MARITA GOLDEN: What was it like growing up in the shadow so to speak of your father's bookstore?

PEARL CLEAGE: When he founded The Shrine, the first one in Detroit, part of their programming was all about politics and registering people to vote, but also about culture. He was always bringing writers in. There were always cultural conferences, and he would bring in so many writers from the Black Arts Movement, which is when I got to meet all these people, Don Lee [Haki Madhubuti] and Nikki Giovanni and LeRoi Jones [Amiri Baraka], who would be coming to speak at my father's church. The bookstores really grew out of his understanding of and commitment to developing artists at the same time as he was trying to develop political leaders.

MG: So you grew up around books.

PC: And also frustrated writers. My mother, my father, and my stepfather all wrote and all wanted to write more than they were able to. They were also trying to make a living and raise their families. They were people who wanted to write, and admired good writing, and admired Black writers who were good writers and also had a certain political perspective. So that we had lots of books by Black authors in the house all the time.

MG: How did all this affect you as a writer?

PC: I think it makes such a difference if you want to write as a Black person if you not only have books in the house, but if there are books written by Black authors. Then it's not something mysterious and exotic to you. My parents never told my sister and me that there were any books we couldn't read, not even a book like Simone de Beauvoir's *Second Sex*. Because my father was so involved with the Black Arts Movement, it wasn't unusual at all for Nikki Giovanni, who was not that much older than I was, to pull up in front of The Shrine [a church and bookstore], coming from Cincinnati with her books in the trunk of the car and Haki would come from Chicago. They all had their little poetry chapbooks that had been printed by Broadside Press.

MG: What were you reading as a child? What were some of your favorite books?

PC: Everything. I read everything. I think probably as a little child, as a young child, the books that made the biggest impression on me that I was reading were the Laura Ingalls Wilder books, all those *Little House on the Prairie* books. They were wonderful because we lived in inner-city Detroit, so of course we didn't know anything about the prairie. I didn't see the prairie until a couple of years ago. But these little girls were so familiar to us in that they were two sisters and doing all these things. My sister actually is the person who turned me on to these books.

So I loved all of those. And the *Cousin Kate from Budapest* books were important to me. I think that part of what I was looking for—because I was always in all-Black environments, consciously all-Black environments, as well as the very radical political family that I was raised in—was books that showed me something different. I already had a Black identity. I was looking for stories about little girls doing interesting things, and most of those were little girls who couldn't have been more different than a little Black girl growing up in Detroit. But it was interesting to me looking back at it because I didn't need that kind of reinforcement of, you should be proud that you're Black. That was what we got from the cradle. We had always had that, surrounded by family, surrounded by people who were always talking about it. So I was reading and looking for little girls with a sense of adventure.

MG: Did you write as a child?

PC: (Laughs heartily) Oh, always. I always wrote. Before I enrolled in school, my sister taught me how to read, and I got a little notebook that my grandfather gave me and I started trying to write my stories. I must have been about five and I was writing little stories and poems.

MG: I think writing can be a calling because like you, I've been writing from a very, very early age, almost as a way of just being in the world. I read, so I write.

I've always had a need to interpret what I saw as a story, to make it a story. It really is a part of how I move through the world, a way of understanding it. There are things that I know I can't understand unless I can write it down.

PC: It's almost like you can't understand it unless you write it down. I remember telling stories to my sister when I was . . . I must have been two because I was in a crib, and I was leaning over the side of the crib—she was already in a twin bed—telling stories to her. And she actually stopped and listened to me tell these stories, which I love her for. But I think that I've always had a need to interpret what I saw as a story, to make it a story. It really is a part of how I move through the world, a way of understanding it. There are things that I know I can't understand unless I can write it down. Because I knew writing was what I wanted to do very early on, it worked in tandem with reading, and both gave me a parallel life, a place where my imagination could be fully engaged and a place to live lives different than my own.

MG: What other books made an impression on you?

PC: My mother was reading Langston Hughes's *The Big Sea* to us when we were so young; it was like it was a real gift to me because not only was it wonderfully written but contained such beautiful stories. It made being a Black writer a real thing to me. I loved the scene of Langston Hughes at Sandy Hook throwing all his books in the water because he was ready to live his life and tell his own stories. The idea that writing was something that I could actually do, that it wasn't just a far-off kind of a dream, was very powerful for me. It was like, okay, this is what I'm going to do. Now all I have to do is figure out a way to make a living while I'm doing it because my parents were very practical people.

MG: Did you ever read the second volume of his autobiography, *I Wonder As I Wander*?

PC: Yes, I did. I loved that. Don't you love when he's in Russia going to these places where they've never seen a Black person? And they really were curious about him, and he was curious about them, and the language became—they had to figure out how to talk since he didn't speak their language and they didn't speak his. I think both of those books were so important to me because they placed Hughes in the context of the whole world while he was so specifically an American Negro writer. He couldn't have been more grounded in who and what he was. But in no way did that ever feel to me like it put him in a little space.

MG: One of the things I like about your books is that you take on contemporary issues and deal with political and social problems. Is that a conscious choice for you, of melding the personal and the political in your stories and in your plays?

PC: I think it's conscious, but I also think that I don't really know any other way to do it because I grew up in such a politicized environment. The whole idea of being a writer was always put forward to me by my family as, yes, that's wonderful, you should get good at it, be a good writer if you're going to be a writer, but also that whatever choice you made about what you were going to do professionally had to be grounded in the struggle of Black people to be free. There never was a space to say I'm just going to be writing as an individual. It was always connected to the community of people.

MG: You obviously did not find that oppressive.

PC: No, not at all, because I think my own life reflects that. I've always been an artist, and I've been an activist, so that I never felt like that in any way confined me. For example, there's always a love story in my books; people are trying to make the community safe, they're trying to get rid of the gangsters and they're also falling in love because I don't find it necessary to separate struggle from personal fulfillment and passionate romance.

MG: As an artist and activist you clearly believe writing is universal because it breaks down barriers between people.

PC: That's right. Look at those Maxine Hong Kingston books, *The Woman Warrior* and *China Men,* just great books that I loved so much. Actually there's only four or five stories to tell. There's the family story. There's the mother-and-daughter story. There's the father-and-son story. There's the neighborhood in peril story. But it doesn't matter what country you happen to be in. These stories are all the same, and people are, I think, generally, unless they're psychopaths, looking for the same thing, which is a place to live in peace, to have their families, to fall in love, to sit on the porch, drink wine, all of the stuff that people do when they're not fighting each other. I think the older that I get and the more that I think about what's happening in the world, the more you really can see that the stories we're telling are the same stories. I think *The Kite Runner* is a perfect example of that, because so many people read that book who didn't know anything about Afghanistan at all.

MG: How is writing a play different from writing a novel, just in terms of structure? And do you find one more satisfying than the other in terms of writing?

PC: It took me a while to get comfortable writing fiction. I'm trained as a playwright. I majored in playwrighting at Howard. They had a Fine Arts program at that time, and my major was Playwrighting and Dramatic Literature, which was great because I didn't have to take any biology. I could take Shakespeare. So that was really wonderful. I like the fact that writing a play is a fairly solitary experience like any writing. You have to finally stop talking about it, actually write it down, find a publisher, and hope somebody reads it. But then once you have written a play, it's a very communal experience where you've got actors, and designers, and directors and all of that. Then you have the terror and the wonder of having the audience come in, so you get to see whether or not it's working, because if it's working, everyone laughs at that joke in Act II. Everyone weeps when the heroine is in distress. When you're in the theater, you see it and hear it with other people. You experience it communally because you're all sitting there together in the dark looking at those other human beings up there in the light. It's a very ancient, ritualistic thing, which really appeals to me, especially as a minister's child because I'm used to ritual and to being a part of the congregation.

MG: What are some of the books and the plays that have influenced you?

PC: I think if I could only read one book over and over for the rest of my life, *The Big Sea* by Langston Hughes is the one that I would pick. It's written with so much clarity and is full of the love that he has for the people that he's writing about and for the life he's living. It's just so wonderful to me that I never get tired of it. My husband is from New Jersey, and he knew that I loved that book. So we were driving on a trip somewhere, and I said, this is not the way we're supposed to be going. It turned out he was taking me to Sandy Hook, which is off the Jersey Shore, so that I could see where in the first scene of the book Langston threw all his books overboard. And I wept. I was like, oh my god, this should be a shrine. The Black Arts Movement was a big influence, too, all of those young writers who were coming to my father's church and bookstore for readings, all of their work was very important to me. Nikki Giovanni, and Sonia Sanchez, Don L. Lee [Haki Madhubuti], and all of them, because they were writing about the same kinds of things that I was writing about and thinking about. They weren't that much older, and they were doing just what Langston was doing, which was fully embracing a writer's life. They were driving these little raggedy cars around with books in the trunk, and talking to people, and really trying to reflect people's real lives in the work that they were doing.

MG: Which plays impacted your writing?

PC: Lorraine Hansberry's *A Raisin in the Sun* had a touring company that came from New York after the play had closed in New York, and I was still in Detroit then. I was a kid. They did it at a high school auditorium and my parents took me and my sister. The auditorium was packed. It was just a regular high school auditorium, but people were all dressed up. The men had ties on and everybody had on church clothes because this play was a big deal, so we all went to see it. It was a wonderful cast from New York, and everybody in the auditorium was just enthralled. You could have heard a pin drop. At the end everybody jumped up and gave them a standing ovation. I had been writing these little plays that I was talking about before, but when I saw that one, it really made me know not only that I wanted to be a writer, but I wanted to be a playwright because I wanted that moment. I wanted the moment where everybody gets to feel it together. I know that's from being a pastor's child and seeing everybody react when the sermon is really good. Everybody's right there. And it was the same way with that play.

I also love Tennessee Williams. I think it's because of those flamboyantly dysfunctional women in the center of all his plays. They're so wonderful to me. You know that those women are really him on that stage! The fact that his characters were so passionate about everything and so confused and so full of secrets that they were trying to keep hidden, makes his plays about *all* our families. Henrik Ibsen is a wonderful playwright who was a big influence, for the same reason I think that the writing was so wonderful. The things he was dealing with, in plays like *A Doll's House* and *Ghosts*, such big social issues, but in a way where you could really look at those people.

MG: He melded the personal and the political.

PC: Exactly; it's like the women's movement slogan about the personal always being political. I believe that's true. The other thing that I think was so important to me as a young person growing up in an unapologetically Black nationalist environment was that my parents never tried to keep me from reading books and plays that were not Black American. They never segregated our cultural experiences. We saw everything and read everything that we wanted to, which I think is a gift to a child because it makes the world bigger, and I think what writers really need to be able to see, is that the world is a huge, complex place.

MG: What are some of your other favorite books?

PC: *The House on Mango Street* by Sandra Cisneros, and *Woman Warrior* and *China Men* by Maxine Hong Kingston. And I think everyone should read Barack Obama's *Dreams from My Father*. I love how in that book he doesn't hide anything, and it helps humanize someone who is in many ways a larger-than-life figure. It's inspiring to everyone.

MG: What gifts have reading and writing given you?

PC: I think they kind of both do the same thing for me, which is to help me make sense of the world. I think I'm drawn more to fiction than nonfiction because the nonfiction is just telling me more about what the world is, what it seems to be. Fiction is telling me more about what it feels like, what the human beings are doing in the midst of all of this stuff. I don't think I could make sense of my own personal life or of the wider world around me if I wasn't writing. I really can't imagine it. Reading fiction always makes me feel hopeful, even if it's a sad story, because the stories connect us as human beings.

MG: Tell me about the play you wrote in memory of Coretta Scott King, *A Song for Coretta*.

PC: It premiered at Spelman College when I was teaching there. When she died, she was lying in state at Ebenezer Baptist Church, and I turned on the TV to see just the regular six o'clock news, and it was cold, wet, dank, not the kind of night we usually have in Atlanta. It was awful weather. But people were standing outside that church all the way around the block waiting to go in to just pass in front of the casket. Nobody was fussing. Nobody was angry to be standing out there in the rain. The reporter was standing in front of them talking, but you could see the people talking to each other, sharing umbrellas, all that.

I remember thinking to myself, because I knew her— actually my first job when I came to Atlanta was at the King Center, so I had known Mrs. King for years—how much she would have really appreciated not only that people came, but that they were really there in a way that was very different than the feeling that people had about Dr. King. It was a much more personal kind of feeling to me.

So when I looked at that, as a playwright I was inspired by that visual. Ebenezer has the cross outside that's neon and then just the little low wall that's in front of it. It was very theatrical where they were standing. So I decided I wanted to write a play about some people who were standing in line waiting to see her, so I made up five women. If you've ever had to wait in line for something, you know that once you stand there for like five to ten minutes, that becomes a little community for that short amount of time that you're in that line.

MG: And you can find out all sorts of things.

PC: They're never going to see each other again, but they kind of confess for that moment. So I had five characters. There's one who's about our age who was really disappointed in young people, just really can't deal with the pants off the behind, rap music, all that. She's really angry about it, which I hear a lot from my friends, and I keep wanting to say, you have to figure out a way to talk over that, to talk around that, to figure out how to hear what these kids are trying to say. But I have that character present.

I had a young woman who was seventeen, pregnant and unmarried and just everything that this older woman really does not approve of. I had a student from Spelman who wanted to do a piece on NPR on these people standing out here, so she's always trying to get people to talk into her microphone.

Then there's a character who survived Hurricane Katrina

whose house and whole block are gone. She lives in her car. She was sitting in front of where her house used to be and just decided to just drive up to Atlanta to pay her respects to Coretta.

Then the last character is a young woman who is in the military who had been in Iraq and she has to go back to Iraq, so she's coming there because she has a Mexican friend who is always praying to the Virgin of Guadalupe. And this girl, the soldier, in my play says, well, we don't have the Virgin of Guadalupe, but I figure Coretta is as close as we've got, so she's there to ask Coretta to look out for her.

It was really fun for me because I hadn't written a play in a long time, but when I saw that line in front of the church, it was like I saw the complete idea. Usually it takes a while to write a play, just like it does a book, but this one I wrote like in a week. It was all there.

MG: You channeled it.

PC: I really feel that too, and I haven't written many things where I felt like, let me get someplace and get still and write down what I'm hearing in my head.

MG: I'm sure that like a lot of Black writers you have some concerns about ensuring that young African Americans become the next generation of readers of your books. What argument would you make to a young person in favor of the book over a computer game, for example?

PC: I'd tell them that a book requires you to slow down, to think deeply and you get to create images in your mind that spark your imagination with books that is very satisfying and that can change your life.

MG: When you look at your life, would you have ever thought that just by being totally committed to these two endeavors, reading and writing, that you would have received so much in return?

PC: Well, no, I could not have imagined some of the experiences, the places I've traveled because of my writing. When I was a child, writing and reading allowed me to join the grown-up conversation at our dinner table, conversation that was always so vibrant, and alive with controversy and opinions. And as I grew older, I became aware of how they gave me the confidence and the perspective to be a part of the ongoing conversation not just in the city where I was born, but around the world.

PEARL CLEAGE RECOMMENDS

The Big Sea by Langston Hughes

China Men by Maxine Hong Kingston

The Woman Warrior by Maxine Hong Kingston

A Raisin in the Sun by Lorraine Hansberry

The House on Mango Street by Sandra Cisneros

DAVID LEVERING LEWIS

LEWIS's contributions to the full understanding of the richness of African Americans' role in the cultural and political history of America has earned him a place as one of this country's most respected historians. The author of seminal works of biography and history, Lewis is most widely known for two overlapping but vastly different texts.

WHEN HARLEM WAS IN VOGUE is a riveting history of the Harlem Renaissance and a definitive book on that era. The personalities, the passions, and the genius of the shapers of that unique blast of creativity are rendered against the backdrop of the unfolding of all the larger historical trends that made the *artistic movement possible. Lewis won two Pulitzer Prizes for his monumental biographies of W.E.B. DuBois,* W.E.B. DuBois, 1868–1919: Biography of a Race *and* W.E.B. DuBois: The Fight for Equality and the American Century 1919–1963.

Lewis's research on DuBois, who lived to the age of ninety-five, engaged him in fifteen years of research. Behind such a grand and productive obsession clearly lay a love of questions, language, writing, and books. Lewis is the author of a dozen works of history and biography.

Lewis's parents created an intellectually stimulating environment for their son. His mother, Urnestine Alice Bell, was a teacher and a librarian; his father, John Henry Lewis, Sr., was a theologian and a graduate of the Yale Divinity School.

We talked one late morning in his Manhattan apartment, surrounded by ceiling-high wall-length bookshelves. The life of the mind, and the life of his mind, was all around us. Lewis's wit and the breadth of his curiosity about all things historical made our conversation wide ranging and energizing. While African-American history is Lewis's intellectual foundation, he is clearly a historian's historian. Lewis is the Julius Silver University Professor and professor of history at New York University.

Marita Golden: I read that you met DuBois as a child.
David Levering Lewis: Yes, it was a brief meeting, just

for a second there. It was at the annual conclave of Sigma Pi Phi, known more popularly as the Boulé. This was in 1948, when I was twelve. My father was like DuBois, an early member of this exclusive African-American fraternity. DuBois delivered his famous Talented Tenth: Memorial Address at that meeting held at Wilberforce University.

To the great consternation and embarrassment of the family, I couldn't read . . .

MG: You clearly seemed destined to write about him. What were the attractions for you of this larger-than-life figure?

DLL: Well, his penchant for reinvention of himself. For me as a biographer, a man who was as principled and as contrary as DuBois is a wonderful challenge.

MG: His life is symbolic of the way that biography and history are conjoined and perhaps inseparable. That in a way they may be the same thing.

DLL: Yes, and it's seldom that you have a life that spans the greater part of the twentieth century and that is emblematic of so many issues that are central to our time, and that continue to be even now.

MG: What were your earliest experiences with books that shaped you as a reader, and possibly as a writer?

DLL: I was not able to read until I was six or seven years old. To the great consternation and embarrassment of the family, I couldn't read . . . and so, I was sent to a Catholic school in Little Rock, and the nuns, of course, were not very compassionate about my stupidity, so then I was homeschooled for a time, and that didn't help. It did have one benefit, that my mother, a teacher, shoehorned in a lot of attention and time for me, and she would read to me, or tell me stories. And so, although I couldn't read, by the time I started to read, I already had this fount of wonderful fables and stories in my head.

MG: What were some of those stories?

DLL: Folk tales like Uncle Remus and Br'er Rabbit, classical stuff out of Greece. My mother was a classicist, and she had excelled in Latin at the old Atlanta University, and she taught Latin, so there was that input. Then we left Little Rock; we were forced to leave, of course, over a civil rights issue and moved to Wilberforce, Ohio.

MG: What was the civil rights issue?

DLL: It was the first major success in the South in the equalization of teachers' salaries. The young Thurgood Marshall argued that case, in 1947, and my father was the principal of the high school in the suit, and he, to the surprise of almost everyone, served as a witness for the NAACP's case. He was summarily fired, and so we moved to Wilberforce, where my father was to become the dean of the School of Theology. So on our way, my mother said something like, "You *must* read when you go to the new school." The new school was the preparatory elementary school of the prep school at Wilberforce. The first day, I was introduced and I was asked to read, and I read, and so I began reading as a result of not embarrassing the family, and after some curious delay in the inability to read.

Since my mother was a librarian, the day I finally began to read was a triumph for us both.

MG: What was the impact of all those stories your mother read and told you?

DLL: Well, it was that I expected information to come in rather vivid ways.

MG: When I was young, my father used to tell me bedtime stories, but he told me bedtime stories about Cleopatra, Frederick Douglass, Sojourner Truth. So I learned at a very early age subliminally that a narrative was a story about a person who does extraordinary things.

DLL: I think that I would echo that, yes, that the story was significant because significant things have happened, and one person probably was the explanation, although I do recall that, for some reason, I was always told by my mother how important the slave narratives were.

MG: Now when did she have these conversations with you about slave narratives?

DLL: Quite early on. In fact, I once said something that embarrasses me today. I said somewhere that I could never get the point of Black history at first because we got it at the dinner table. As an example, my mother had gone to Tuskegee one summer, and took a distinct disliking to Booker T. Washington. She would bring this up at the dinner table. My father, who was more pragmatic, would point out that Washington had his redeeming features, and so on, but he was a DuBois fan, so this is just part of the mix of things. And a whole range of important African-American leaders passed through our home, because of course there was no hotel that

African Americans could stay in in those days of segregation and so the local families would offer them room and board. My family felt that it was their obligation to house everybody, so it was a wonderful asset for a would-be biographer.

MG: Who would some of the others be?

DLL: There was Reverdy E. Ransom, a charter member of the Niagara Movement, senior bishop of the AME church, a spellbinding orator, and a Wilberforce neighbor of my family's; my mother's first cousin Archibald Carey, Jr., who was an alternate delegate to the United Nations appointed by President Eisenhower; Walter White, who was head of the NAACP, and also distantly related; and then all the AME bishops in the world, of course, to my mother's despair, because of the enormous amount of cooking that was entailed (laughs gently).

MG: So you were literally feasting at the feet of these historical figures.

DLL: Or people who thought they were historical figures.

MG: Once you started reading on your own, what kind of experience was it for you?

DLL: It offered me solace and solitude. We had a library, my father's study was full of books, and on the wall, in addition to his sheepskins—one from Yale and one from Chicago—were these panoramas of the Acropolis and of the Coliseum.

So, I can just remember sitting on the floor, reading and looking up at this stuff, and letting my imagination roam, and then pulling off the shelves volume after volume of history from the beginning of time to the present. Everybody it seemed was on those shelves; there were French and German historians and I'd pull them down, and just cull a few pages, and lose myself in the history of great White figures.

I read to my predilections, which were, as you were describing, significant lives doing significant things.

MG: You read mostly, you know, the history of the world through White male eyes, but were there Black history books that you read as a child?

DLL: There were discussions of one man, quite a bit, and that was J. A. Rogers.

MG: Oh, yes, my father was a devotee of his and had all of his books.

DLL: My parents would argue about whether Rogers was nuts, or whether he was to be credited.

MG: Which parents took which side?

DLL: My mother would be very, very skeptical. My father would be rather more endorsing, but both found it delicious that he had outed Beethoven and Alexander Hamilton, and the Brownings, writing about their Black ancestry. So that was just part of breakfast conversation, from time to time.

MG: What specific books or authors have meant the most to you at different points in your life?

DLL: I always find that question very difficult. They certainly are there, but I have trouble with an inventory. I first read *The Souls of Black Folk* very early on.

MG: You say early on, your late teens, or . . . ?

DLL: No, before that, I think by the time I relieved my parents of the embarrassment of not reading, I got *The Souls of Black Folk*. So, whether or not I sat down and I read all sixteen essays at one fell swoop, or whether this was just by osmosis,

I'm not sure. My parents were unabashedly pro Talented Ten-thers. They took no trust with any criticism that DuBois's idea was elitist or snobbish or anything like that. They thought that people who had education and some resources automatically had obligations, and had to be conscious of their responsibilities to others.

MG: Yes, and you had to have a leadership class, whether you want to acknowledge it or not.

DLL: Exactly. Surely one of the earliest books that influenced me was *The French Revolution: A History* by [Thomas] Carlyle.

MG: And how old were you when you read that?

DLL: I must have been about ten. On its pages was a description of the attempt of Marie Antoinette and Louis to escape from Paris, and reach the Austrian frontier, reach the Austrian army, which is ready to march and restore them to power. They get into a large carriage called a *berline* with about six horses pulling it, and they get into it in downtown Paris in the Hotel de Ville. They go out a side door, and the Marquis Lafayette leads them out; they get into that carriage, and they head for the frontier of their country. Carlyle gives the reader a breathtaking sense of the momentum of this vehicle rolling up and down hills as it's going, and what is happening in France, and the people who discover that the king and queen had fled. Everybody realizes now it's serious business. And at the end, just as Louis is within two miles of the Austrian army that his wife's brother-in-law has sent to save them, he sticks his head out of the window, and a peasant recognizes him from a coin. He is apprehended and brought back, and of course, the guillotine. Even as a young reader I knew that's the way to write history, and so, it affected me deeply.

MG: You were hooked.

DLL: I was absolutely hooked. You could get the rhythm in the language, so that Carlyle's ability to replicate motion in prose was so admirable. So that was certainly one book, and then William Edward Burckhardt, a Dutch historian. And then, somewhere along the line came the Durants, Will and Ariel. I read everything they wrote, and we had the books in the family library, and this would have been just as I was getting ready to go off to college.

MG: What did your youthful reading in a larger sense connect you to?

DLL: To other people, and I found that with my peers, I was a great storyteller among them, and often found myself in a leadership position because I would invent things that we had to go and do, charging off in various places amidst the rural setting of Wilberforce. My imagination was really pretty fervent.

MG: You were part of a unique environment in your pre-college education; what was it like at Fisk?

DLL: I went to Fisk University at fourteen or fifteen, and so, as my wife says, "You had the advantage of never growing up. So you don't know what life's about." To some extent this is true. There we were, sixty kids—thirty women, thirty men in this Ford Foundation program that was the most enriched curriculum I suppose you could imagine.

MG: It was the first of its kind?

DLL: Yes and it was modeled on the University of Chicago's

program; it was a genius program, and the reason it was established was that Charles Johnson was able to persuade the Ford Foundation that so much of education in the American South was wasted because of the inequalities in resources.

Therefore, the first exam, which became the SAT, was the Fisk exam. And if you passed that, you entered Fisk, fully funded for three to five years, depending on the rate at which you proceeded, and the faculty was a faculty that was created to service this population. They came from Harvard and Yale, and the historian August Meier, it was one of his first jobs, and David Granick, the economic historian of the Soviet Union. . . .

MG: These were your professors.

DLL: These were my professors, and Bob Hayden, the poet laureate, and, oh, the man who had great impact upon us all, certainly me, was Aaron Douglas, the art professor.

MG: With professors of this caliber you were in academic heaven.

DLL: Yes, I was.

MG: How has the act of writing, spending so many hours writing, and being a writer, shaped and enriched your life emotionally, intellectually?

DLL: For me writing history has given me a wider perspective on things, I think. I was really mindful of that, as an illustration, when the whole business of immigration exploded several years ago, when we just went wild about it. I gave a talk at NYU. I gave the baccalaureate address at NYU, and I just said, "Let's have a little history. We've been this way before with the Jews and the Italians and the ethnics who were 'polluting our republic,' and so, we closed down Ellis Island in 1924."

MG: Really?

DLL: Yes, the Jones Act shut down Ellis Island, because we thought, anymore of these people, and we will lose it. The real America will go, and I said, in my talk, "So, here we are again. The real America is about to go. By 2020, the country will be brown, California will be totally Hispanicized, it's the end of civilization as we know it." Well, let's step back and say, "Who is saying this, and what is really the case, and what did happen," and I think historians have that kind of perspective, but I think, also, novelists would, as well. You—I mean it is absolutely an axiom, that to understand the present, you have to have a context, and the context is the past, so there's that.

MG: Of the books that you cited, that meant so much to you, and you know, all these other books that have been seminal in creating you as a historian, is there one book—

DLL: Oh you mean the what-would-you-take-on-a-desert-island question? Well, I'd have to say, I'd have to say maybe in three fields there have been particular books that I would choose. One book for the American experience, one book for the diasporic experience, and one book for the rest, the European. For the American experience, I think Richard Kluger's *Simple Justice* is one I would take with me.

MG: Why?

DLL: It seems to me it reconstructs how we won *Brown versus Board of Education*. How we put that together, and it's by a White journalist, but his treatment of Thurgood, and of

Charles Hamilton Houston, and the players in that is just wonderful.

MG: Have you read it more than once?

DLL: Yes. Yes, I have.

MG: What are the different things that you see in it, each time you've read it?

DLL: Well, I guess—and let me back up and say for that kind of reprise that deepens, it wouldn't be Kluger, it would be Tocqueville's *Democracy in America.* With DuBois, it's all over the place, there's no one thing that quite captures him. Yes, I think *Dusk of Dawn.* I think that is just extraordinary. So I'd take that, because it comes out in 1940, and it's true, the last Pan-African Congress is yet to happen, but everything has happened. I admire the intellectual imperiousness of *Dusk of Dawn* and DuBois's statement that he practically invented the modern Negro people. Then for the European experience, Stendahl's *The Red and the Black,* DuBois's *Dusk of Dawn,* and Tocqueville.

MG: Why does Tocqueville last?

DLL: Because he saw first what the experience of democracy in this country was going to be like. Somebody smart being first to make the observations, that's DuBois's story, too. Tocqueville said it first. And as an aristocrat, he had a kind of skepticism of democracy. He could see that the tyranny of the mass, the tyranny of the majority is as great a danger as the tyranny of the tyrant.

MG: Why *The Red and the Black*?

DLL: Because psychologically it's so wonderful. You get into the head of General Kutuzov.

MG: Who is a character in my favorite novel, *War and Peace*.

DLL: I admired Tolstoy's wrestling with and dramatizing the perspective, really, of men in war, that they really just do not have a clue about the large picture in which they're going to lose their lives, or in which nothing makes much sense.

MG: What is your favorite book that you've written? Is it DuBois?

DLL: No.

MG: Really?

DLL: I do love *When Harlem Was in Vogue*. I think it's almost a perfect book in terms of the craftsmanship, the density of the research, and what I'm trying to say.

MG: Do you see signs of the impact of the decline of reading in your students?

DLL: Yes. Oh, yes.

MG: Even with the overachieving students that you're working with?

DLL: They don't read—reading is different now. Undergraduates are coming with an innocence that is petrifying. They don't know anything except what their elite high schools gave them. But they have no history, and they have no sense of connectivity to anything.

MG: What did their elite high schools give them?

DLL: Well, whatever they did, they did well. But since the competition to get into NYU and these places requires you to have a profile in which you've done brain surgery, and you've swum with the whales, and been to Africa, and all that, they are exhausted. Now, technically, they can write pretty well, and this technology allows them to retrieve information, and so they stumble into plagiarism through Wikipedia, and through downloading, and cutting and pasting.

MG: If you were going to meet any historical figure from the past, or the present, who would it be?

DLL: Well, I'll be really perverse, and say that I would have liked to have met Che Guevara.

MG: Why?

DLL: I read Jon Anderson's magisterial biography of Che, and he just appeals to me on all sorts of levels. He was credentialed as a physician, had a first-rate mind, determined to make a great difference, radically. To stand the world on its head, and to put those convictions to the test with an AK-47 in the steamy jungles of Angola, or to stand up against the Great Satan, the United States, in Latin America. I just think it's wonderful. I would have loved to have had a beer with him, and to have listened to him talk.

MG: Do you think people will always read books?

DLL: Yes, I do. Just as they'll always listen to the radio, always read, I hope we'll always have newspapers—they're having a hard road to hoe, but, yes, I think so. There is nothing that will replace it. Nothing, nothing will replace it. I cannot read the newspapers or books onscreen, won't do it. I want to decorate my space with books.

MG: Do you have a telling or funny or interesting anecdote or story that somehow reveals your relationship to books and writing, your passion for it, or your connection to it?

DLL: Well, I'd say two stories come to mind. When I was a finalist for the National Book Award in 2000—no, in 1994, that was the first time—the news was carried in the Rutgers

University newspaper and it said, "Rutgers Professor in the Lead in the NBA." So, in the instant of miscomprehension, people I had never seen, you know, came running up to me and said, "We didn't suspect that at all."

MG: They thought you had a secret life as a professional basketball player and had no awareness of the National Book Award, that's a good one. What would you tell students about the importance of the kinds of knowledge we gain through books and how that knowledge has affected your life?

DLL: Reading the kinds of books I've spent my life reading promotes independent thinking and the betterment of the mind, and books offer the permanent possibility of traveling anywhere at any time in any age. That's what I've spent most of my life doing.

DAVID LEVERING LEWIS RECOMMENDS

Silent Spring by Rachel Carson

The Lives of the Caesars by Suetonius

The Ways of White Folks by Langston Hughes

Black Jacobins by C.L.R. James

The Rise and Fall of the Third Reich by William L. Shirer

Black Reconstruction in America, 1860–1880
    by W.E.B. DuBois

War and Peace by Leo Tolstoy

Remembrance of Things Past by Marcel Proust

The American Language by H. L. Mencken

NATHAN McCALL

The publication of Makes Me Wanna Holler: A Young Black
Man in America *was a publishing and literary phenomenon.
The book, which chronicles the coming-of-age journey of journalist Nathan McCall, struck a nerve in the African-American
community and among such a diverse audience that the book
topped the* New York Times *best-seller list for weeks in 1994.*

*Against the backdrop of intense national concern about the
rising rates of homicide among Black males, the book possessed a
nearly prophetic force and an undeniable authenticity in the midst
of the midnineties media-generated discussion about the plight of
the Black male, a discussion that was often full of more heat than*

light. At the time of the book's publication, Nathan McCall was a reporter for the WASHINGTON POST *who wrote with unflinching candor about his struggle for identity, his youthful involvement in crime, his incarceration, and how he found and created both a voice and a positive, new life. The book was a powerful story of loss and redemption. Since its publication,* MAKES ME WANNA HOLLER *has attained the status of a perennial best seller. It is the kind of book that its fans give to those in need of inspiration and guidance. It is the kind of book that evokes passionate testimonies about its ability to change lives.*

Like Malcolm X, McCall found himself and his possibilities in prison. Prison is where he became a writer and a reader. Prison is where he discovered writers who impacted him in the manner that his book now affects others. I interviewed him in his home in a suburb outside Atlanta. In a wide-ranging discussion that covered everything from the dark side of integration to what he learned about writing from Flannery O'Connor, Nathan talked about how and why writing and reading are life-long journeys that have enriched his life.

MAKES ME WANNA HOLLER *was followed by a book of essays,* WHAT'S GOING ON, *and most recently a novel,* THEM. *Nathan has come a long way from the Portsmouth, Virginia, working-class neighborhood where he grew up. He teaches African-American studies at Emory University in Atlanta.*

MARITA GOLDEN: Were there any surprises for you in writing *Makes Me Wanna Holler,* things you learned about yourself you had not expected to confront?

NATHAN MCCALL: I realized in writing the book that as a teenager I was deeply depressed. And there's nothing more dangerous than a depressed Black man because we don't express our depression the same way that a lot of people do because of a lot of the macho values that we internalize and one of those values is that I would be less than a man to kill myself. But I can kill somebody else or get them to kill me and it would be a more acceptable death.

MG: I don't get the sense in the earlier parts of *Makes Me Wanna Holler* that as a child you were reading that much, or were you?

NM: No.

MG: But when you got into prison, things changed. Why?

NM: Well, anybody who has spent twenty-four hours in a jail cell can tell you that it's maddening. You get in touch with aloneness on a level that you never had to deal with before. And that happened for me. In jail they used to have this cart that came around, and it was full of books. That might be your only diversion for the day. So I would poke my head out and look. That's how I ran across *Native Son.* I was looking at this stack of books and one had a Black man's picture on the cover. So I picked it up and said, "Let me check this one out" and began reading. And it was like, whoa. I had never seen anything like that before. When I started reading about Bigger Thomas, the protagonist in *Native Son,* it was like, whoa.

MG: Did you feel that Wright was talking to you?

NM: Absolutely. I was Bigger Thomas all the way.

MG: You were Bigger Thomas?

NM: All the way. He was suicidal. He was depressed. And he had this sense that there was this larger world out there that he had to go into, he was being pushed into. It would be like being pushed into a boxing ring with handcuffs on, and the opponent and the referee are going to kick your ass.

I had never been pulled into a book like that before. It just made me cry. I remember I finished it at about three o'clock in the morning and I was just weeping. After I read [*Native Son*], it was like, damn, I didn't even know somebody had written something like this.

MG: Now in the prison library, was there a good selection of African-American literature?

NM: Actually there was. Then I ran across, of course, *Malcolm X*. Then I ran into other brothers who were reading and they began recommending other books, George Jackson's *Blood in My Eye, Soledad Brother, Soul on Ice* by Eldridge Cleaver.

MG: So you were turned on to these books by fellow prisoners.

NM: Both. When the cart came around, I would check the cart and see what else was on there. Then I probably talked to some of the guys about what I read and then some of them, they were on their second or third bids [jail sentences], so they could recommend books. Then there was the regular prison stuff like Donald Goines. I read all of Donald Goines's stuff. Any time somebody tells me they've read Donald Goines, the first thing that crosses my mind is, how much time did you do?

And so I went from reading this story about Bigger Thomas, which got me thinking about my own life, to journaling, and that's how the writing started. I started writing down what I was feeling. I needed to get it outside.

MG: Did you have a notebook?

After I read [Native Son]*, it was like, damn, I didn't even know somebody had written something like this.*

NM: Yeah, I had a notebook. You could buy little things from the canteen, and I bought a notebook and started writing down what I was feeling. Prison ain't exactly the best place to be telling somebody your deepest feelings, talking about your pain. So I was writing stuff down. And I realized that it made me feel better, whatever I said, whether it was a paragraph, whether it was a page. Sometimes I would just write, and it would be disjointed and everything, but it would make me feel better. So the more it made me feel better, the more I did it. Then the more I did it, the better I became at it. Then I began to see it became a challenge to get my feelings down with the depth and preciseness that I felt.

MG: You're talking about the transformative power of reading and writing, that a book can change a life, save a life, inspire people to find themselves. What would you say to young people, who are as alienated from the process of education today as you were in your youth?

NM: I would say that they should not be intellectually passive, that they should read and write to ensure they get a good education. Most of the best books I've read were NOT introduced to me in school. So I would encourage young people to go out and find literature that speaks to them to supplement what they get in school. That way they will really get a so-called good education. I was fed a lot of Shakespeare in school, that while useful, primarily reinforced White supremacy and did not speak to my experiences as a young Black man.

And so that's why one of the reasons that prison becomes a place that so many Black intellectuals discover themselves, is because it is enforced, imposed aloneness. That's what reading requires, aloneness. So suddenly people who would not be still long enough to read are forced to be still in a jail cell. You can only count the ridges in the wall so much before you reach out and try something new. When that book cart comes around, you look for something.

MG: I'm at a point in my career where I am really aware of how much writing is a gift to people, and it's a gift that keeps on giving.

NM: Oh, no doubt. A book is permanent. Before I left prison I had decided that I wanted to become a writer, and it was based in part on the fact that I advanced from writing a journal to coming alive intellectually, and beginning to experiment with all types of writing. We formed a writing group, and one of the prison counselors served as our supervisor. We would write everything, even poetry.

MG: Was there ever a kind of "aha" moment when you realized in a definitive way the power of the written word?

NM: I remember one day being in the prison library and reading this article that sealed it for me. It was an article that was about a conference that was held somewhere in the world where a group of historians had come together and tried to decide who was the most influential person throughout all of history, and they did a poll to see who people thought it was. Most people said Jesus Christ, of course. Others said Prophet Muhammad. They came up with about eight people in the poll. The historians said, no. You know who they said was the most influential person throughout all of history?

MG: Who?

NM: Gutenberg.

MG: The man who invented the process of printing from movable type.

NM: When I read that, it was like, wow. That's powerful. What that article did for me was that it connected the dots in terms of how someone like a Richard Wright could reach me even though he was dead and gone, or how he could reach me and he wrote in Chicago, how he could make me cry and he was in Chicago and I was in Virginia. And so ever since then I've been real clear about the power of writing. It was just a matter of how I was going to pursue it.

MG: Other than Richard Wright, what other writers affected you profoundly?

NM: Oh, there's a whole list. Angela Davis. I went through all of them, anybody who would put it out, DuBois, after the lightbulb came on. I think everyone should read *The Prophet* by Khalil Gibran; I have many favorites, including *Blood in My Eye* by George Jackson, *Animal Farm* by George Orwell,

Madame Bovary by Gustav Flaubert. In reading, one thing leads to another. One book will make reference to another book, and then you say, well, okay, I didn't know about him, or, I didn't know about her, let me go check her out. And in prison I had the leisure to read up on people until I was thoroughly satisfied.

I remember I was on my Gwendolyn Brooks thing, going through her. And I wrote to her. I wrote to her after reading her stuff and said, I really like your stuff. I'm in prison, blah, blah, blah. And damn if she didn't write me back and send me a book of her poems called *Aloneness*. She helped me understand the difference between loneliness and aloneness, which helped me negotiate that prison experience even better.

MG: So obviously, reading and writing allows you to connect with people spiritually?

NM: Definitely. It helps me connect with writers whose work I ingest, especially if the writing impacts me deeply. As well, it amazes me when I read novels and connect with a character on a visceral level. That's one of the most exhilarating experiences there is. In a sense I've connected with two people, the writer who was able to pull off such a feat and the character. And as a writer I get the spiritual connection in reverse. Readers who connect with my writing often contact me to say how my work has impacted their thinking, or even their lives.

MG: So prison became a kind of intellectual incubator for you?

NM: I have a theory that in prison you can put together your own intellectual diet, which essentially is what I did. In school, you are subjected to a curriculum that has an objective, which is propaganda. Miles Davis, I remember reading this interview once where he said he could always tell when he was listening to jazz if there was a White musician in the band. He said if there was a White musician playing, the music just wouldn't go in his body. When I was in school, a lot of what they were teaching, it just wouldn't go in my body. So when I discovered Richard Wright, it went in my body. That's what happens to some people when they go to prison. They discover the literature that will go in, that they're often not exposed to in the school system, and they're not exposed for a reason because it is literature that will encourage critical thinking. It is literature that may not support the myth of America. And they don't want Black folk thinking.

MG: Do you journal every day?

NM: No, not every day. Sometimes I might say, wow, it's been two months now, I need to get back to my spirit if I feel myself coming unglued, not centered. Sometimes I need to document, just say, what is happening. But I still need to journal because life still happens, and the journaling, I can't have enough conversations about what's going on inside of me.

MG: Where does your inspiration to write come from?

NM: Literally from everywhere. I can listen to music and be moved to write. Other times, I read about issues or events in the newspapers and it affects me emotionally on some level or inspires me to think more deeply about some idea. That's what happened with my novel *Them*. I read a newspaper story about a conflict in a Black neighborhood where African Americans were concerned about Whites moving in and taking over. After reading the article I tried to imagine the nature of the conflicts that would erupt as a result of Blacks and Whites suddenly finding themselves next-door neighbors, even as they were cultural strangers and mistrustful of each other.

MG: Now when you turned to fiction, what was the challenge around turning from nonfiction autobiography to fiction?

NM: I was reading books on how to write a novel. I started off with that. Then I studied novels. I would read something and then dissect it. I would read a novel and then essentially break it down, put a file in my computer on that novel where I would outline the structure to see how the person did it. I would look at how they developed character, how they did that story, where they put it, that kind of thing, what they did with voice. Then I studied voice. I looked at Flannery O'Connor in particular, who represents southern White rural voice. I had to get clarity about the voice of the characters in this book, which I decided had to be a mix. I wanted southern Black urban and southern Black rural. Then there was generational voice. I've got one character who is of this generation, hip-hop, and another character who was more old school. I worked to try to capture the nuances of voice. That part was fun, but it was the structure piece and the characters that was challenging. And then the other challenging piece for me was because I feel so passionately about race and how it impacts our lives, I knew I had to set out to write a book and at the same time restrain myself from wielding the sword.

MG: Not writing propaganda. Writing a real novel.

NM: That's right. With each book I have written down

goals that I want to achieve. With *Makes Me Wanna Holler*, the goal was to be brutally honest, and so there were times I had to check myself.

MG: There was a point in that book where I had to put it down. I said, is this Negro crazy? But then the testimony to the success of the book is that I picked it up and continued reading.

NM: In the novel, that's where my journalism training really, really helped. The journalism training helped because I was able to sort it through in the same way that we do as journalists. As journalists, we see something that interests us and then we explore it. And this whole issue of gentrification piqued my interest and I wanted to explore it. As journalists, once we gather some information and we decide whether it's going to be a straight news story or whether it's going to be a feature. Once I gathered some information, I decided that this could not be a nonfiction book, that it had to be fiction.

MG: Why?

NM: Because I was writing about race relations and the impact of gentrification in the Black community and if it were done as a nonfiction book, I think probably four people would have read it and three of them would have been my family members. It's just not a sexy topic as nonfiction, number one. Secondly, I thought about my audience and how we receive information. Quite often what I saw with *Makes Me Wanna Holler* is that I could feed people intellectual ideas if I slipped it into a story.

MG: You make your political points through drama.

NM: So you have to figure out a way to do it so readers

don't feel like they're doing heavy lifting. That was one of the reasons. The other reason is this, that I knew that if I did it as nonfiction, I would probably need to go around and do a lot of interviews—interview White people, Black people, and all that. And as journalists we've learned that when you interview people about race, they quite often don't tell the truth. I may or may not have gotten to the truth.

MG: And there's a higher truth. There's an emotional truth that's active in a story.

NM: That's right. And so with fiction I knew I would have the flexibility to take readers inside people's heads in a way that I might not be able to do with nonfiction. I felt confident that since I have studied race, and had conversations about race with all different kinds of people, that I could approach this with a degree of authority. And so that's why I decided I need to try it as fiction.

MG: What advice would you give to an emerging writer?

NM: The first piece of advice that I would give is that they need to gain clarity about whether they want to become a writer or whether they want to become published. There's a difference. I run into a lot of people who simply want to see their name in print, and it's not the same as wanting to be a writer. And I have very little patience for people who simply want to be published.

MG: Because anybody can get published these days.

NM: And for some people, it's not about wanting to be a writer. It's about wanting to satisfy their ego. To see their name on a cover. My advice for people who are serious about writing is to read everything that is there, to study not only writing but writers. One of the things that I've always done, and I did a lot in prison, that helped me, is that I would read biographies of people to understand how they structured their lives. I would read about writers to figure out what they do when they get up in the morning. What did Hemingway do? Where did he write? What were the problems he encountered? At one time I could have been a Richard Wright scholar because after I read *Native Son* I read all of his stuff.

MG: I also talk to people about creating a life environment that supports your writing, so that you're going to have to get rid of some people in your life who are naysayers, who don't believe in you.

NM: I call it spring cleaning.

MG: Once you make the decision to commit yourself to this endeavor, it changes everything in your life. It's not just about what's on the page. It's about your whole life, and that's what people often don't realize.

NM: I also tell people to be honest with yourself about whether you have a writer's temperament. A writer's temperament, number one, is relentless. It is, I will do however many drafts as are necessary to get this right. What is necessary. So my advice is to go through the checklist first. Number one, figure out whether or not you just want to see your name in print. Go and pay a printer to do five thousand copies and make yourself feel better, and send them to some family members, and be done with it. But don't say you want to be a writer. The other thing is check yourself to see if you have the writer's temperament to go through this. It means spending time alone. It means structuring your life in a certain way. It means being able to live two lives simultaneously.

MG: Inside and outside.

NM: Also writers have to be lifelong students of writing, different kinds of writing, different authors. Sometimes I'll take one author and read everything that they've done because that teaches me what themes they keep coming back to. It teaches me voice. I begin to see repetition in characters. I begin to see how they work certain things. I've always admired Sidney Sheldon because he wrote most, if not all, of his books, from the point of view of the protagonist who was a woman. And I wondered if I would ever have the confidence to be able to write, to even pretend to be able to get in the head of a woman? In *Them* I had to do it with a major character. I think I was able to do it, but I don't know yet that I'm ready to do a whole novel with a woman as the protagonist.

MG: I think writing is an intellectual challenge that is very satisfying. It is hard. It is a challenge. And you don't know what you're writing until you start writing. You don't often know until you've finished.

NM: One reason I like watching sports is that I study it as a metaphor. The athletes that reach the highest plateaus are those who pay the biggest attention to detail. Tiger Woods for example, and Michael Jordan, back in the day, he paid attention to detail. I remember Phil Dixon said something to me once that I have never forgotten. He was my editor briefly at the *Washington Post*. When editing a story I'd written he'd say, "You need to get more work out of that paragraph." And as soon as he said it, I understood what he meant. That there are some people who can say in a paragraph what it takes someone else three pages to say. And it's because they understand nuance and the power of precision, using that thesaurus to get the right word to express the right emotion in the right way. That's the difference in flat writing and rich writing. So my advice to people is be clear that if you really want to write, then you've got to be prepared to suffer.

MG: The life of the writer is more than a notion.

NM: *So much more* than a notion.

NATHAN MCCALL RECOMMENDS

Their Eyes Were Watching God by Zora Neale Hurston

My Name Is Asher Lev by Chaim Potok

Things Fall Apart by Chinua Achebe

Paris Trout by Pete Dexter

The Autobiography of Malcolm X: As Told to Alex Haley

MAT JOHNSON *was the prover-*

bial lackluster student whose indifferent academic performance masked a fine mind, an insatiable curiosity, and a talent for writing that was in hibernation. Born and raised in Philadelphia, Mat has defied his own early expectations by receiving an MFA in Creative Writing from Columbia University, traveling in and writing about Europe and Africa, and penning five highly praised works of fiction and nonfiction. His first novel, DROP, *was a Barnes and Noble Discover Great New Writers selection; his second novel,* HUNTING IN HARLEM, *won the Hurston/ Wright Legacy Award. And he has delved into nonfiction with a book about a New York City slave revolt,* THE GREAT NEGRO

PLOT, *and is now contributing to the graphic novel genre with* CONSTANTINE HELLBLAZER: PAPA MIDNITE *and* INCOGNEGRO.

One of the most seductive qualities of Johnson's writing is his gift for humor and satire, and he blogs on subjects including Black Nerds, Mulatto Issues, and Humor Writing. Our conversation covered everything from how waiting forty-five minutes for a bus to get to school made him a reader, to why his favorite book of all time was written in the 1860s, to Toni Morrison's influence on his writing. Johnson is a member of the faculty of the creative writing program at the University of Houston.

⌇⌇⌇

MARITA GOLDEN: I've heard you make fun of yourself, about how you were indifferent to reading and scholarship as a child. Talk about that and how you suddenly changed and became a reader.

MAT JOHNSON: My mother read all the time. She would read a novel every night. But I didn't read. I was addicted to television. I didn't even want to learn to read actually, and my mother had to force me to read. I remember she wanted to read Dr. Seuss's *Snow* to me and how she chased me down the steps and held on to my legs, and I screamed that I didn't want to listen to it. Eventually she bought me comic books. I think that was the first time I was kind of interested in actually figuring out what the characters were saying.

MG: Was it the visual aspect?

MJ: Yeah, I think that's part of; it made it less threatening. I think as an adult, less threatening means more paragraphs, but as a child it's seeing pictures. And honestly I read comic books almost primarily as a child until I got to the point where I had to actually pay for them myself. I needed to read because of public transportation, sitting and waiting for the bus for forty-five minutes, an hour, and you'd have nothing to do. That's what made me a reader. Then I started reading books that were superhero comics and then I began reading science fiction books, books by Piers Anthony, and Rogers Zelazny, and all these science fiction writers. Then I kind of stayed in that pattern up until high school. Around that time I remember listening to Public Enemy in the eighties and hearing them talk about Malcolm X, and that made me interested in reading *The Autobiography of Malcolm X*. I saw some kid at school had it, and I picked that up, and that book opened up the world of intellectual African-American dialogue. So I went from that to *The Souls of Black Folk*.

MG: What I hear you also saying is that there was kind of a back and forth between a lot of different media so that television didn't keep you from reading, and music enticed you to read, which is very interesting, particularly when I think about young people today who are hooked into so many different types of media.

MJ: I wonder if I'd had an iPod with a video screen, would I be a voracious reader?

MG: That's the question a lot of us are asking.

MJ: When people started walking around with video screens everywhere, I thought to myself, that's going to be the real challenge for books now.

MG: Do you think there can be a happy medium so to speak, between books and the types of visual and social media being developed at what seems to be a breakneck pace?

MJ: I'm hoping it's possible. The truth is that TV tells one type of story, and a good book will tell a different type of story. I tell my students that watching something on TV is like having a public conversation and reading can be like being in the closet in the dark with somebody whispering into your ear. It's so much more intimate.

MG: What are some of your favorite books?

MJ: There's a bunch. I think the three favorites by the end of high school were *Song of Solomon, The Autobiography of Malcolm X,* and *The Souls of Black Folk.* Although I was a horrible straight-D student, I was reading on my own all the time. I had read all of Morrison by the time I went to college. My teachers saw me in the hallways and at lunch reading these books that were on a reading level that was really advanced, so they ended up forming a reading group that included some students, administrators, some of the secretaries, and a couple of the teachers.

MG: What was the name of the school?

MJ: This was Abington Friends School. A Quaker school. I had gotten kicked out of public school, and my dad rescued me and got me into this Quaker school. And so I went there for junior and senior years, which didn't improve my academics. It was just quieter. I just kind of read more. I used to sit in Spanish class and just read my books, which is why my Spanish is as poor as it is today.

MG: Tell me more about the book club.

MJ: Well, they must have wanted to like rescue me, so they formed this group, and it was like eight of us, and we had a book club, and it was outside of regular class. I read *Catch-22*. And I had never really read a satire before. And so that just blew me away. I liked the book because I saw in it a reflection of all the hypocrisy that was starting to be very evident in the adult world that I was getting closer to but nobody was acknowledging. I basically talked about *Catch-22* all day and drove everybody crazy with it for about six months. Then another book I was reading was Charles Bukowski's *Factotum*. I think as a high school student once again I related to the book because, like *Catch-22*, it gave me the feeling that the universe is a lot darker than adults were telling us. The plots of his books are pretty basic, man gets drunk, man does bad things, and then passes out. But at the time having an adult talk like this was really exciting. But here we have stories with nothing much happening, but the way he was writing it, the language was intriguing and pretty seductive.

Sometimes I think, if not for books and all that reading I did, I would have ended up as the bitterest person at the customer service office at Philadelphia Energy Company. I was destined for it. That's where I was supposed to be. I was supposed to be answering phones at PECO smoking Newports, and living a life of monotony. The nice thing about books is you get to see the possibility of other realities. And that's really exciting.

MG: With the current emphasis on standardized testing in the schools, the reading of books and in-depth writing seems to have been marginalized. What would you like to change about that?

MJ: I'd give students books they want to read about the subjects they want to read about, written in the most sophisticated manner they can handle. Young people care about stories, creativity, and having their voices heard.

Sometimes I think, if not for books and all that reading I did, I would have ended up as the bitterest person at the customer service office at Philadelphia Energy Company.

MG: Do you believe people are, in general, reading less than in the past?

MJ: Actually I think people are reading more than ever, just in different forms—on Facebook, texting, tweeting. The question is about the form of the story. But I know that the stories will outlive any trends in reading or publishing. The art will always continue. I have faith in that.

MG: So books were a refuge. They were escape. They were an incubator for your latent talent as a writer and an intellectual.

MJ: You're exactly right.

MG: So you went to London on an exchange program in your junior year?

MJ: Yeah, I went to Wales.

MG: And that was the basis for your first novel?

MJ: Yeah. That was my first international experience. By the time I finished up as an undergrad, I learned how to get As, and I ended up getting a scholarship called the Thomas J. Watson Fellowship. And so I went back to London, and I also was in Ghana, West Africa, for a while. The point of my fellowship was actually to look at how and why so many Black writers had been changed by international experience. The school gave me like $24,000 to basically run around the world for a year.

MG: What did you do, research, interview people, write a paper?

MJ: I basically interviewed a lot of people. I asked them why they're abroad, how they had changed, how they were a different person. The inspiration for this inquiry was books like *Malcolm X* first, and then looking at the works of James Baldwin. And that's why I ended up in Ghana. So it was kind of trying to access that world. But while I was in London I fell in love with a woman, we got engaged but the whole thing went to hell, and I came back to the states and ended up working at the electric company in Philly just like I was supposed to in the first place, and that ended up being the inspiration for my first novel, *Drop*.

MG: Was there any one writer who more than others opened up new possibilities for you once you began to write?

MJ: Toni Morrison's work told me that you could create entire worlds and you can create entire realities, and that was extremely attractive. Now she's become like the mainstay, but in the eighties when I was first reading her it was like she was creating a new universe. And then when I got to Ralph Ellison, I remember that was a big kind of wake-up call. I'm looking right now, I see the book right on the shelf, the one I had in college. I came late to class because I had to finish the whole book, I couldn't put it down. When I got to Ellison I saw similarities between his *Invisible Man* and Joseph Heller's *Catch-22,* they both had this way of looking at the absurdity of the world and using that as a social criticism, and not just like a straight political criticism, but a criticism of humanity. That just blew me away.

MG: What are the unique pleasures in a very personal sense for you of reading?

MJ: I think right now the unique pleasure for me, besides the utter indulgence of having the time to read, which is a pleasure in itself, is the possibility of reading an entirely new voice, an entirely new way of looking at reality. When I read a voice that's different, I can feel my brain just expanding.

MG: And the unique pleasures of writing?

MJ: Everytime I think I know who I am, when I write, I get to smash that. When I wrote *Drop*, I had one concept of who I was as a writer, and when I wrote *Hunting in Harlem,* I could smash that and do something else. When I write, it's the ability to evolve with a new project. It's a clean slate. It doesn't matter what you wrote last time. It's what you're going to write this time. You don't get a lot of clean slates in life.

MG: Who would you recommend to somebody who wanted to graduate from reading purely commercial fiction?

MJ: I would tell them that if they have an interest in mysteries, go read more sophisticated mysteries, ones that you're going to get more out of. So if you like mysteries, start reading Walter Mosley or Chester Himes.

MG: If they enjoyed books about love and relationships, they could read *Their Eyes Were Watching God.*

MJ: Right. I think you come in for one thing with a book often. You come in for the subject matter. You come in for the prose. You come in because you know the author. Then if it's a good book, you discover other things that you like, and then hopefully you kind of swing from vine to vine by doing that.

MG: What writer from the past would you like to have dinner with?

MJ: That's an easy one. Frank J. Webb.

MG: Who is?

MJ: He wrote *The Garies and Their Friends.* It's a really odd book, and it's the second novel written by a Black writer in America. It was written during slavery, right before the end of slavery, but it's not about slavery. It's a book about Black people for Black people at a time when everybody was writing propaganda. And because of that, it just was completely ignored. I mean, Harriet Beecher Stowe actually wrote an intro to the book, and she just has no idea what the hell she's talking about. It's comical when you read the actual book because she just thinks it's an abolitionist text. To me Webb was the first obscure Black writer, and he was the first Black writer I think who wrote primarily, who wrote a book primarily for Black people.

MG: What would you ask him?

MJ: First, what the hell was he thinking? I mean, talk about trying to aim for obscurity. I'm just fascinated. The thing is, the whole point of the book is stay within your community. Don't leave. Don't worry about White people. Just take care of your own. And if you step out of your community, that's when you're going to get hurt. What he's talking about is basically what the *Cosby Show* ends up talking about in the eighties, form your own middle-class world where you take care of yourself. It's just so far ahead of its time. And the funny thing was, he was in Philadelphia; the book is set in Philadelphia when he wrote this, and he ended up leaving Philadelphia and moving to Galveston, which I just took my kids to yesterday. So I've kind of ended up following the pattern of his life. And the book is good. It kind of also shows me that there are a lot of good Black writers who, because they don't fit in politically or whatever, become obscure. But then it also taught me later that that doesn't matter. The point is you write a good book, and this book is one of the best I've read.

MAT JOHNSON RECOMMENDS

The Autobiography of Malcolm X: As Told to Alex Haley
The Souls of Black Folk by W.E.B. DuBois
Song of Solomon by Toni Morrison
The Garies and Their Friends by Frank J. Webb
Catch-22 by Joseph Heller
Factotum by Charles Bukowski

JOHN HOPE FRANKLIN

was one of the world's most revered and respected historians. Born in 1915, and named for John Hope, an important African-American educator, John Hope Franklin lived a life devoted to groundbreaking scholarship and public service. The author of more than twenty books and hundreds of scholarly articles, Franklin, at the time of his death in 2009, was the James B. Duke Professor Emeritus of History at Duke University. In 2000, in honor of Franklin, the university opened the John Hope Franklin Center for Interdisciplinary and International Studies.

Franklin's impact on several generations of Black historians is unparalleled. Professor Henry Louis Gates said on Franklin's death, "He gave us young Black scholars a common language to speak to each other. He had invented a genre out of whole cloth." Pulitzer Prize–winning historian David Levering Lewis said that when he was deciding to become a historian, news came that Franklin, his mentor, had been named department chairman at Brooklyn College. "Now that certainly is a distinction. It had never happened before that a person of color had chaired a major history department. That meant a lot to me. If I had doubt about the viability of a career in history, that example certainly help put to rest such concerns." Lewis also said that while researching his biographies of W.E.B. DuBois, he became aware of Franklin's "courage during that period in the 1950s when DuBois became an unperson, when many progressives were tarred and feathered with the brush of subversion. John Hope Franklin was a rock; he was loyal to his friends. In the case of W.E.B. DuBois, Franklin spoke out in defense of an intellectual to express ideas that were not popular."

Franklin was the author of many award-winning books but is perhaps best known for FROM SLAVERY TO FREEDOM: A HISTORY OF AFRICAN AMERICANS, *a text that is continuously updated and is a staple of African-American history courses. His other books include* THE EMANCIPATION PROCLAMATION *and* THE MILITANT SOUTH, 1800–1861. *His autobiography,* MIRROR TO AMERICA, *won the Hurston/Wright Legacy Award and is a fascinating account of a man who literally witnessed all the major historical changes in African-American life of the last century.*

I interviewed Dr. Franklin a year before his death, at his home, not far from Duke University, in Raleigh, North Carolina. Our talk began in his parlor and continued over a lunch of shrimp fried rice, during which he showed me an original copy of one volume of the two-volume HISTORY OF THE NEGRO RACE IN AMERICA FROM 1619–1880 *published in 1883 and written by America's first great Black historian, George Washington Williams. As an early fan of this historian, who was little known until Franklin's biography, I felt chills holding the book in my hands. Franklin spent forty years researching and writing an award-winning biography of Williams. He showed me as well some of the countless translations of* FROM SLAVERY TO FREEDOM, *in languages from Japanese to French. We talked about his childhood in Oklahoma and the years in which his parents were forced to live separately as a result of the Tulsa race riots, a tragic event during which several hundred African Americans were killed, his view that African-American history and American history are one, and the books and writers who influenced his life as a writer.*

MARITA GOLDEN: How did you decide to write your autobiography, *Mirror to America*?

JOHN HOPE FRANKLIN: Well, I've reached the age where if I didn't do it, I was afraid someone else might and although I have no objection to people writing about me, I thought I should have the first opportunity to do the writing and give them some concrete, accurate information about myself and what my experiences have been. So I undertook the writing.

MG: What did it give you personally to write that book?

JHF: Well, it gave me an opportunity to be self-critical, to make some judgments as to where I had gone right and where I had gone wrong. It also gave me an opportunity to reflect critically on what I might have done to others or to society, whether I was on the mark or not, to take stock, make inventory.

MG: You have had such a rich professional life, and have been involved in so many endeavors that changed society, how were you able to recall as much as you did in the book?

JHF: I saved nothing until I was chairman of the Department of History at Brooklyn College. There I had to save material because I had to make annual reports to the Board of Higher Education, plus the fact that I had two secretaries then. I had no one to help me up to that point, not anyone. And I did everything for myself, and I didn't have time to worry about the record. My wife, who I married in 1940, was a saver; that is, she thought that everything, every scrap of paper was important. We didn't have any agreement on that. I didn't think about saving, so I didn't. So when I got ready to write my autobiography, I had to do research.

MG: On yourself.

JHF: On myself. Someone came into the library once and asked me what I was doing. I said, I'm doing research. They said, on what? I said, me. I had to do it. That's where I make a distinction between an autobiography and a memoir. A memoir I think—this is my definition—is what you remember. You sit down and say, what am I going to remember about myself? That wasn't enough. I can remember a great deal. And I can feel a certain confidence about my memory because I reinforce it with research on the event. I'll give you an example of how I didn't remember something. When I was a kid just getting into high school, I fell in love with classical music, and when I got ready to write about that period in my life, I could not for the life of me remember some of the people who excited me when I was young. I had to go back to read the newspapers, read when the Chicago Opera came to Tulsa, Oklahoma, in 1929 or '30. I remember Rosa Raisa singing and could not remember what she sang until I read it in the paper. I went back and dug the songs out. So I wasn't ashamed to do research and to correct myself in the meantime.

MG: What were the special challenges or satisfactions of writing about yourself?

JHF: Well, there were very few satisfactions. I guess there were challenges, such as trying to be accurate. Trying to be fair. Trying to make value judgments on myself and on my experiences and others.

MG: One of the things that I loved about your autobiography was that you talked a lot about your parents. They were extremely important in encouraging your early reading and your intellectual life. Could you talk a little bit about that and the values that they imparted that really made your achievements possible?

JHF: They made my survival possible. They were a remarkable couple themselves. They were extremely devoted to each other and worked together. My mother was enormously

resourceful. There was a long period when my father was trying to start a law practice in Tulsa and we were staying behind
in Rentiesville [Oklahoma] and were separated for four years.
What my mother did in instilling self-reliance and a sense of
responsibility when we were just tots, to my sister and I was
very important. I was six, she was seven. When we got ready
to move, I was ten and she was eleven. My mother was teaching, what we call, in the mountains. I don't really quite know
where it was. But she went on horseback every day over the
hill, the mountains. But to me, a six-year-old, it was in the
mountains. She went over the hills on her horse, riding in her
saddle, and after she left, we went to school locally. We had
to walk about a half a mile or so to the school. She instilled in
us a great sense of responsibility. It got cold and if it rained,
we would stop in Ms. Collins's house and stay there until she
came. If we went home, we had duties. I had to clean the
lamp, chimneys, and fill them with kerosene. We had no electricity. And my sister and I had to get in the wood. The wood
was chopped, but it was outside. We had to bring the wood in
the house. There was no question about our being safe from
prowlers or burglars. There was no such thing, you see. We
just got home. I don't think the house was bothered, so we just
went in and we did our chores. But no matches. If it was dark,
we couldn't turn on the light because that meant striking the
match and lighting the lamp, and that was a no-no because it
was dangerous. And we had to get our lessons. If we finished
our chores, there was time. We couldn't eat until Mother came,
so we worked on our lessons for the next day, because that's
discipline, you see. My mother, she wasn't mean or strict, but

we just had to do that. That's the way kids were raised in those days. You obeyed. Something to do, you did it. We had a real sense of hard work and industry instilled in us.

MG: What do you remember most about your father during this period of the family being separated?

JHF: My father would come home maybe once a month from Tulsa to Rentiesville. That was about sixty miles or so. He'd catch a train. No automobiles in those days. He came on maybe Saturday and Sunday. And you can imagine what it meant for me to expect my daddy to come home. It was a wonderful time. I think about it now. I'm ninety-three, and I was nine, eight, nine, ten, missing him terribly. I can feel it now. So it was a great pleasure, when he came home, sometimes without our knowledge, without telling us. He'd just walk in. And he taught us a great deal, but he was not there every day. My mother taught me everything I knew as a boy. One of the amazing things about it, even as a boy and she was a woman, she taught me how to be a boy. I went fishing and I did all these things outdoors, under her tutelage.

MG: But clearly your father prepared you to make your transition into adulthood, spending time with you on his job, in his work.

JHF: Yes, after we moved to Tulsa. I was ten then, and from ten to sixteen he was in my life every day. That was wonderful.

MG: Who was an author you read as a child?

JHF: I read Paul Laurence Dunbar. He was very popular. Enormously popular in the first part of the last century. I read novels, children's novels. My mother had a good library for us.

MG: Now your mother was a teacher, your father was a lawyer so obviously there were books in your home, and literacy was very important.

JHF: Literacy was very important from the beginning. There was no debate whether or not you should read and write. You'd better read well and write well. And the reading I did gave me a sense of life beyond the world I was living in. My mother and father had been to college, so their horizons were wide, too, you see. Although they had never been to Europe, they could talk about Europe and the Holy Land and all these other places. So I didn't feel isolated or bound by Rentiesville or by Oklahoma even. The world was big from almost the beginning.

MG: Do you write with a sense of unearthing Black history?

JHF: Oh no. No. No. I don't call myself a Black historian, you see. That's one of my problems. Not that I mind it, but what I've tried to do all my life is to put what I know about African Americans into the larger framework of history. Our history is the history of this country.

MG: So you essentially put African-American history where it really belongs.

JHF: Yes, where it belongs. So I didn't have a sense of mission of writing. You ought to know, too, that I didn't have any sense of mission about anything connected with Blacks until much later in my career. First, I wasn't going to be a historian; I was going to be a lawyer. Then when I decided to be a historian, I was already in college, second or third year in college. And then my history professor, Theodore Currier, was

White, and he wasn't teaching Black history. He was teaching history. And although I wrote a paper called "Free Negroes in Antebellum Tennessee," that was the first time I had an opportunity to look at the place of Blacks in American history. Whatever I wanted to do, he was encouraging me to do it. He didn't have any mission about Black history, and I think for me that was probably good because I never was overwhelmed by Black history. I never regarded that as the only thing in life, you know what I'm saying? Therefore, was able to keep some balance. I had no mission.

MG: Are you saying that as a historian you're looking at the big picture, the whole picture, not necessarily one part of it?

JHF: Well, I think some historians, if I may say so, don't look at it that way. And this is true of African-American historians who get so immersed in African-American history, they lose the big picture and don't make the connection. I don't believe in separating African-American and American history at all. I never taught Black history anywhere, but I taught American history in a way that you couldn't miss the Black history.

MG: What do you think of the history texts that are used in public schools?

JHF: I have a very strong opinion on that, and that is that I think history is poorly taught. The books are written by a committee, and they've got nothing in them except some soft pabulum as I call it. You don't learn much, and that's one problem. The other problem is that at least in my experience, and maybe yours, too, the people that taught history in high school were not trained. They taught it because that was something left over in the curriculum. In my history class, the coach was the historian, and he knew about as much history as this thing here (points to a vase on a table between us). So I thought history was just a joke, and I didn't get interested until I was in college. I wasn't going to do anything with history. That was my position on history when I finished high school. I didn't know what history was like or what it could be like until I was in college and I heard this professor lecturing. I said, is that history? My god, that's very exciting. That's when I began to think about majoring in History. My majoring in History had nothing to do with African-American history at all. It was just a lively field, and you could learn so much from it. How are you going to be educated without it?

MG: What are the books that have most influenced you in terms of your career as a historian? Books that other historians have written or that other people have written?

JHF: Well, I guess the old Edward Channing book *A History of the United States, Volumes 1–6* was what really turned me on first.

Then even as an undergraduate I began to read DuBois. You see, he graduated from Fisk, so he came to Fisk at least twice when I was an undergraduate. I didn't meet him. I just saw him. He was so goddamn arrogant. But I admired him and I read *Souls of Black Folk*. I never got over that. I'm still not over it.

MG: Why haven't you gotten over *The Souls of Black Folk*?

JHF: It's so powerful. It's just so powerful. It is so eloquent.

It's so well done. And the essays, you could put your hands around each one.

MG: What does a book like *The Souls of Black Folk* say to a high school senior or a college freshman today?

JHF: Well, it would tell you what a human being he was and how human beings have things in common.

MG: The interconnectedness of us all.

JHF: When I got to know DuBois many, many, many years later, I found that, despite his arrogance, he never had a true sense of how important that book was. After I moved to New York, he had me come to his class to give a lecture. He was teaching at City College. It was not a full program. He was giving a course. But he was sitting in the back of the room when I'm giving the lecture. That was one of my few greatest hours, that W.E.B. DuBois was taking notes while I'm teaching. That would blow you away, wouldn't it?

MG: Did DuBois influence your writing in any way?

JHF: Oh yes. One always tried to write the way DuBois wrote.

MG: Why is reading important?

JFH: We cannot have independent thinking without being able to read freely. Reading is important if you can pick what you want to read. If somebody is selecting the things for you to read, then you're bound by that unless you are able to do your own thinking in connection with that reading. But that's problematic, and I would say that is important if you're able to read freely, read all points of view. I guess some of the highest rates of illiteracy are in countries that are not democratic.

MG: And if we're going to say that reading, and particularly the ability to choose what you read, is important, what about writing? Is that just as important? Right now public school students are studying, for example, mostly to pass mandatory standardized tests, and the ability to write with skill is declining.

JHF: It's unfortunate that this trend has set in, but I think you're right. We don't value reading as much as we did. It doesn't wield the same power as it once did. We are taking too many short cuts. We're reading, but when we do read, we don't read critically.

MG: Because as a historian you have been asked many times to provide perspective for those building cases for social change, such as the NAACP, and considering your work with helping them build their argument in *Brown versus Board of Education,* would it be fair to call you in some sense a public intellectual?

JHF: I don't mind people calling me a public intellectual as long as I define it myself.

We cannot have independent thinking without being able to read freely.

MG: What is your definition?

JHF: Addressing any subject in a way that it has an impact on the general public.

MG: What is the role of the scholar in society?

JHF: To provide society with the intellectual tools it needs to function properly and successfully.

MG: One of my most satisfying moments as a student was in American history class one day. My teacher started talking about Black history, and he mentioned a certain person as the first historian, the first Black historian. And I corrected him and told him about George Washington Williams. He hadn't heard of him, and I had read a small article about him. Clearly your biography of him is your favorite of your books.

JHF: No contest.

MG: Could you talk about why he's so important and why you spent so many years doggedly making sure that you could write his story? It gave me a huge thrill when I was eighteen or nineteen to know about him, and I didn't know nearly as much as you had written in your book.

JHF: Well, it's my favorite, and I think it's my most satisfying contribution in many ways because he was the person I created.

MG: When you say you created him, what do you mean?

JHF: That he was only a name. I didn't give him a name, but I gave him almost everything else. I knew a name, but I didn't know what that name was or what it was about until I began to ask myself the question, who is this man? I didn't know anything about him. It was in the 1940s that I began to realize that this was something that couldn't be dismissed in a paragraph or in a word, that you had to know something about him. I set out to find out something about him. I began to talk to people. One day I was talking to Dr. Carter G. Woodson, and I asked Dr. Woodson, who is this man Williams? He said he was quite a person. He said he had an extraordinary gift, a deep commitment to scholarship. And he said, if you write a paper on him, I'll put you on the program at the next meeting of the association.

MG: The Association for the Study of—

JHF: Negro History. And I regarded that as a challenge that I should meet, and so I wrote the paper. And in writing the paper, I found out just enough about him to whet my appetite. He had written the history of the Negro race in two volumes. He published it in 1882. It was the first history of the Negro until Woodson wrote his in 1921. Normally the history of the Negro race is in one volume. I said I was going to write about him.

MG: So because of what he had done, the two volumes, that fired your imagination with all types of questions about who he was.

JHF: Yes. I wrote a paper on him first. There was nobody more attractive and exciting and interesting as Williams. I didn't know anything about him, except that little stuff in the *Dictionary of American Biography,* which was about that long (holds up two fingers). And I began systematically following him. The next thing I found was a piece of paper that Williams had written to Oliver Otis Howard, the founding president of Howard University around 1869. He had heard of Howard University, so he wanted to go there, and he wrote a letter to General Howard. This became so characteristic of him. He didn't start at the bottom; he started at the top. And that's the first piece of writing I have of Williams. It's in the papers of the Howard University Library. He wrote to Howard in a letter that I have reproduced in my biography of Williams, some of which I haven't been able to decipher yet, it was so poorly done. Howard really endorsed the letter by saying, admit if qualified. Then I was able to take that letter and work on it. He just said enough in there so I could get some hints. So I go back and really try to reconstruct his life. From that point on I followed Williams, any step he made anywhere. Anywhere he went I went. He went to California, I went. He went to Canada, I went. He went to Europe, I went. Belgium, England. I don't know how many trips I made to England chasing this man down. I reconstructed him as much as I could. He went to Africa, and I went to Africa. My first time going to Africa was chasing Williams. He went to the Belgian Congo. He was the first to blow the whistle on King Leopold for his inhumane treatment of the native people in the Congo in the 1870s and '80s. And so he went to the Congo, and I went to the Congo.

MC: So this was a magnificent obsession. Would it be fair to say that writing this book was like writing none of your other books in terms of your personal involvement?

JH: I was in Williams up to here (holds hands above his head). When he left Egypt, he went to East Africa, and I went up to Egypt, caught a ship, sailed the Mediterranean and back to England. He took this trip in 1881, 1882. And on the ship he met a woman that he liked, lived with her, I guess, for the rest of his life. And in England he also got sick and died. He was forty-one or forty-two when he died. In North England I discovered his grave and put a tombstone on it.

MG: You spent decades on this.

JHF: Forty years.

MG: You spent as long reconstructing his life as he had lived it. What did he teach you as a historian?

JHF: He was very careful in his research.

MG: The two volumes that he wrote, where would you find those two volumes?

JHF: Well, I have two sets myself. I have *The History of the Negro Race in America.* I have his *The History of Negro Troops in the War of the Rebellion.* I have about fifteen or twenty pamphlets he wrote on various aspects of life. And I have clippings. He wrote a column for the *Cincinnati Enquirer.* He was the first Black columnist that I know anything about. There's a woman in Brooklyn who read my biography of him and she was so excited about his life that she's writing a play about him and teaching a course in New York on Williams. She's gone to Africa. She thinks she'll go to England. I've never seen anybody be so excited about something I have done.

MG: So it must have been extremely satisfying for you for the book to be met with so much acclaim and recognition upon its publication.

JHF: It was great satisfaction.

MG: How do you look at history, its purpose and meaning?

JHF: Well, I look at history a lot as the human experience

from which we can learn a great deal. And that helps us to avoid mistakes that have been made in the past. That's the importance of history to me.

JOHN HOPE FRANKLIN RECOMMENDS

The Souls of Black Folk by W.E.B. DuBois

Part III

Reading for the Soul

> "A book is a world, a book
> is a friend; that's why
> people love books. A book
> is a marvelous thing. It's a
> person between covers."
>
> —J. California Cooper

THE IDEA OF BEING "LIFTED" IS A RESONANT AND ENDUR-ing concept in African-American culture. Lifted beyond life's travails. Lifted, in Black theological terms, above sin into the realm of redemption. So too, the idea that reading and writing "lift" one and are "good for the soul" is a long-held and potent belief, for those who see reading as a virtue and writing as a blessed form of alchemy.

Whether the book is Saint Augustine's *Confessions*, or Rich-ard Wright's *Black Boy*, we instinctively understand the ability of language to transform our spirits, save and renew our physical and psychic selves, and connect us one soul to another. For the writers in this section, intellectual curiosity and imaginative creation express their souls' deepest yearning and lodge them in the souls of others, where as wordsmiths they feel that they quite naturally belong.

© Ellen Banner

J. CALIFORNIA COOPER

will tell you that she isn't a writer as much as she is a storyteller. Her characters, inevitably inspired by the music she plays when she is writing (it could be classical or it could be jazz), step forth and claim her. Cooper swears that when she sits down to write, it's pure possession; she's merely a vehicle through which her "people" come into being. Cooper's "people" act out artful, entertaining morality tales written in a plain-spoken style. Love, hope, home, and family are the pillars that form the foundation of her prize-winning, beloved stories.

In a J. California Cooper story you feel like you're hearing it in front of a fireplace, over a sumptuous home-cooked meal, or on your grandmama's front porch. The author of more than seventeen plays and nearly a dozen books of fiction, Cooper won the 1989 American Book Award for HOMEMADE LOVE. *Her other works include* IN SEARCH OF SATISFACTION, FAMILY, THE FUTURE HAS A PAST, *and most recently the* NEW YORK TIMES *best-selling* LIFE IS SHORT BUT WIDE.

Novelist Alice Walker encouraged Cooper to write stories after reading her plays. She published Cooper's first book, A PIECE OF MINE, *a collection of short stories, through her publishing company, Wild Trees Press. And perhaps Walker best sums up the quality of Cooper's voice that has made her a best-selling author, and in the view of many of her readers a dear friend, when she says, "Her style is deceptively simple and direct, and the vale of tears in which her characters reside is never so deep that a rich chuckle at a foolish person's foolishness cannot be heard."*

I visited Cooper in her airy, spacious home in Portland, Oregon, where she showed me around the house and told me stories about favorite objects and what goes on in each room. And she briefly donned the famous caftan she wears whenever she reads publicly from her work, the dress in which she becomes and gives life to "her people."

MARITA GOLDEN: California, you were saying when you were showing me around the house that you write to music. What does music give you?

CALIFORNIA COOPER: Music is a stimulant. Whether it's Rachmaninoff, or Dinah Washington or Earl Gardner, it's the mood they put you in. I can never play Rachmaninoff without getting a character, somebody who's talking. And that's how they come.

MG: What else inspires you to write?

CC: The Bible and life, those are my two greatest inspirations, and they have influenced my work more than anything else.

MG: What is your new book about?

CC: *Life Is Short But Wide* is about two old people. I usually write about people no one else is paying much attention to. People always talk about young people falling in love or the healthy, and the beautiful, so I write about the crippled, or the disabled, or the ugly. In this book they got old. She was sixty-three, which isn't old, but it's as far as I could take them, and he's seventy-three. I wanted it to be a gentle love story. The kind of love like you had when you were in the seventh grade, sweet and innocent. You liked that fella, and you got tingles, but you would never tell him. They kind of did that for a long time.

MG: Your books have always struck me as parables or allegories.

CC: When you're writing about one thing, everything comes into it because that's life. That is why I don't like people to fool around editing my books too much because when I put something in a book, I'm looking at it happening to music. It's in my head and I'm watching it happen. Because I don't tell the characters what to say; I listen to what they say, and they do their own dialogue.

MG: It's almost like you're channeling?

CC: Yeah, from whatever wisdom that's sitting somewhere. So I don't like you to change what they say. And everyone doesn't speak alike, so I don't want them to speak like you. I want them to speak like they did. You can correct my misspelling, but do not correct my dialogue because I heard the character say it in my mind.

MG: I'm interested in the feedback that you get from the people who love your work, your fans. What do they tell you that they love about your stories?

CC: That it was like I was talking to them. One fella wrote me from New York. He said, "Everybody in your stories comes into where I work, my bar." Or somebody will say, you must live in my house. They know these people. But to me, reading is for learning. I don't want to read a book that talks about everything I know. When I'm searching through books, tell me something.

MG: Something new.

CC: Yes. Even if you only verify what I already know and it's in a different way, I'm still learning because we all know everything about whatever they put in these books. Women and men meet and they fall in love, or in like, or in lust, and they have sex usually, and it's not right, and so it doesn't turn out right, and they're arguing about jealousy and lies. So what else can you put in a book? That's why gossip doesn't appeal to me although people love it.

MG: Books are enormously powerful, aren't they?

CC: I tell young people a book is a mind, it's somebody's brain you're meeting. The author of the book is preparing you for life. A book is a world, a book is a friend, that's why people love books. A book is a marvelous thing. It's a person between covers.

MG: What has your religious faith given you as a writer and as a creative person?

CC: Well, in my books I try not to ever lie and I knew that Jesus Christ came and died to save us, but I didn't know why His blood saved us, why He was a ransom until I became a Jehovah's Witness.

MG: As much as faith and religion is important to you, you don't mind having your characters use profanity.

CC: There's not a lot of it, but if the word fits, that's what they say. And also sex. That's in there because that's life, and that's the problem they're having, so I can't leave sex out because they don't.

MG: Did you get a lot of encouragement in your home growing up in Berkeley, California, for your creative gifts?

CC: Well, I don't think any of us knew I had them, but my mother loved to read, so even if she was cooking, she was reading. So I developed this love of books. And once you read, how can you get enough?

MG: What did you read as a child?

CC: Everything. When I did get a library card, I was so

happy that I could go to the library and get a card and take books home. And they let you keep a book for two weeks. But in a year or so, I had aliases at the library.

MG: You were using other people's library cards?

CC: Well, I had to get new cards because they didn't ask you then for your birth certificate and everything or your address. So you just go in and say, "I'd like a library card, please," because I had so many of them.

I tell young people a book is a mind, it's somebody's brain you're meeting. The author of the book is preparing you for life.

MG: Oh, because you were so late in bringing the books back.

CC: Oh yes, because you fall in love with the stories.

MG: So you didn't want to bring the books back.

CC: And didn't have the money to buy them.

MG: Well, when I was a kid, the library was almost like church to me. It was a sacred space. What are some of the books that have meant the most to you?

CC: All of Pearl Buck's books, Taylor Caldwell. Isaac Singer taught me how to take life and make it a great story. I love *Meridian* and *The Third Life of Grange Copeland* by Alice Walker, Zora Neale Hurston, and *The Bluest Eye* by Toni Morrison.

The Ten Commandments is my favorite part of the Bible.

It's at the heart of everything we do, every mistake we make, greed, covetousness, everything.

MG: Definitely. I read an article that said that you played with paper dolls.

CC: Until I was eighteen.

MG: What did you like about paper dolls?

CC: You could tell a story. That's what it was. And I loved the stories. The fact is they were paper, so they couldn't do it without you. It was the fact that you had somebody who could stand up there and say, "Oh, Howard, don't do that." My mother said you could put me in a room by myself and shut the door, and you would think a crowd of people were in there if you didn't know that I was in there by myself because I talked to myself.

MG: And you were never alone when you were in that world of your imagination.

CC: Right. That's why when I was eighteen my mother got scared that I was retarded or something. It was time to put the paper dolls down. That's why the first thing I ever wrote was a play. I couldn't play with the paper dolls anymore, so it was he said/she said. Even before I was old enough to write I was telling stories through paper dolls. I could see life, and I paid attention to it.

MG: That's a great statement, that you could see life and you had to pay attention, because that's what a writer has to do, pay attention.

Did you ever take any writing courses?

CC: No and in school I failed in almost everything except maybe English, and in math I was horrible. I got so many

Ds, barely passing only because the teachers liked me. They wouldn't give me an F. They said things like, you see, Joan [her first name], she will be able to get a job any time in her life because she has personality.

MG: When you started writing the plays, how did the plays begin getting produced?

CC: That was years later when I was grown, and my daughter took them to the Berkeley Black Repertory Theater. I was never going to show them to anybody because if you told me those plays were lousy, my heart would have been broken. So I never would have sent anything. I never have sent anything in, never, because I can't deal with the rejection of my work, my people, because I love these people that come to me in these stories.

MG: How many years had you been writing plays before your daughter took them to the Black Repertory Theater?

CC: Oh, maybe about twenty years. I thought how nice it would be if they were produced, but I didn't know if they ever would be. But I thought they'd be really good. I never took seriously the idea of making it as a writer. But I always worked.

MG: Where did you work?

CC: I worked as a credit manager at Berkeley Credit Union, and I worked as a loan officer at Fidelity Savings and Loan and Beneficial. I got good jobs because of my personality.

MG: So in what year was your first play produced?

CC: It must have been about 1981, '82.

MG: And is that around the time when Alice Walker approached you?

CC: Yes, she came to one production in San Francisco,

the Berkeley Black Repertory, and then they took the plays to UC-Berkeley and everywhere. Then they spread out.

MG: I understand that you write in long hand?

CC: I have to use long hand. The minute I step in front of something mechanical, my characters disappear because they don't like it. If I just write long hand, it's like it can flow, right? But the minute I step in front of a typewriter or computer, it's gone. I type it later but do my first drafts in long hand. The computer ruins all your imagination. It's mechanical, and that's what stopped me, the mechanical part of it. My thing is total imagination. And if you mess with the imagination, you just put a block in my way. So that's why I'm always dying to write some stories that I really want to write, but they're more ephemeral. They follow the feelings. Sometimes your feelings take you to a place that you don't want to talk about. I'm awfully shy, and I have written stories that I'll never show to anybody.

MG: Writing for publication is a relationship with not just your characters and your ideas, but it's a relationship with your readers. Is there anything you've learned from your readers?

CC: I realized that they really liked the wisdom in my stories and the fact that reading them they could feel like they were with their grandmother or their mother, and they could hear some of those same words. By that time, I had gone through another metamorphosis because I was listening to reviewers and to people who were considered intelligent, and who were telling me about my books, saying you could speak much better English than that. We have to bring our people up and all that shit. And what my readers liked about my books is that it was what they knew and what they liked hearing from their grandmothers, from the past, in that kind of language. They liked that. And also White people liked it because it was authentic.

MG: Yes, and their grandmothers and fathers spoke the same way.

CC: Yeah. I had one reviewer once, ask who is this woman using all these exclamation points in her stories? And I said, my people don't live in periods; they live in exclamation points.

MG: So your readers have given you affirmation of your instinct to write from the unexpurgated, unchanged wisdom of your characters as they come to you. When you're trying to write the way critics want you to write, that's where you go off. So your readers are smarter than the critics.

CC: I had good characters in the books, but they talked too much. In fact, when I was reading one I said, this book talks too much. My first books, the first three or four books I wrote, they got to the point.

MG: So you had to struggle to hold on to your authentic literary voice.

CC: Fight for it.

MG: One of my favorite books of yours is *The Wake of the Wind*. Since it is essentially a saga covering several generations, I'm interested in your research.

CC: I read books, but I didn't research.

MG: Now what's the difference between reading books and researching?

CC: I read Black history books and all that sort of thing, but I didn't make notes and I didn't plan to use the information. I knew from the Bible that the only thing that's changed in life is clothes. People have not changed. And that's all I write about is people, so I didn't think about all the environment and all that.

MG: But you had great details.

CC: I got them from my characters. My characters or looking around them or just knowing something. One lady asked me once at a newspaper, I think she was in Cleveland or Denver and she said, and what sort of research did you do for *Family*? That was my first novel. And I said, research? I said, listen, what would you want if you were a slave? What would you need to research?

MG: What is your favorite book that you've written?

CC: Well, I love *Some People, Some Other Places,* but I also love *In Search of Satisfaction,* and I loved *The Wake of the Wind.* But that's the same way you love your children. They're different, but they're all wonderful to you. I don't like the book because of anything I did that made it; it's because the people made it. That's what makes these books good.

MG: What do you think has been the most significant development for Black writers since you started writing?

CC: The most significant change is that they get published, and I know that sounds oversimple. But when I was living in San Francisco like around '80, and I went into the Black bookstore, Marcus Bookstore, and I saw all those books, that was the first time in my life I ever realized that Black people really wrote books. But that really hit me hard, and I realized I was very pleased. And even more than pleased, I was just bowled over. Now it doesn't only have to be the man who has the money and the education, ordinary people can get published if they have something to say.

J. CALIFORNIA COOPER RECOMMENDS

Meridian and *The Third Life of Grange Copeland*
   by Alice Walker
The Bluest Eye by Toni Morrison
The works of Pearl Buck, Isaac Singer, Zora Neale Hurston,
   and Taylor Caldwell

CHIMAMANDA N. ADICHIE

With the publication of two highly acclaimed novels and the recent short story collection THE THING AROUND YOUR NECK, *Chimamanda Ngozi Adichie has become one of the most mature and promising young literary voices coming out of Africa. From her debut work, Adichie exhibited a poise and depth in her writing generally associated with veteran writers. Born in eastern Nigeria in 1977, Chimamanda's first novel,* PURPLE HIBISCUS, *about a family struggling to survive under the brutal hand of an evangelistic father and husband, won the Commonwealth Writers Prize for Best First Book and the Hurston/Wright Legacy Award. Her second novel,* HALF OF

A YELLOW SUN, *about the Nigerian–Biafran War in the early 1970s, won the Orange Prize for Fiction, one of Britain's most prestigious literary awards.*

Chimamanda's father was a deputy vice chancellor at the University of Nigeria, Nsukka, and she grew up in the house that famed Nigerian writer Chinua Achebe and his family had once lived in. At nineteen, Chimamanda left Nigeria and moved to the United States. After studying at Drexel University in Philadelphia, she transferred to Eastern Connecticut State University, from which she graduated summa cum laude. She then received an MA in Creative Writing from Johns Hopkins University and an MA in African Studies from Yale.

The title HALF OF A YELLOW SUN *refers to the Biafran flag, which was the symbol of the Igbo region of Nigeria that broke away from Nigeria's central government. Having lost both her grandfathers in the war (they died as refugees having fled from their hometowns), Chimamanda has said, "I grew up in the shadow of Biafra. I grew up hearing 'before the war' and 'after the war' stories; it was as if the war had somehow divided the memories of my family. I have always wanted to write about Biafra—not only to honor my grandfathers but also to honor the collective memory of an entire nation. Writing* HALF OF A YELLOW SUN *has been my tribute to love: the unreasonable, resilient thing that holds people together and makes us human."*

Chimamanda was preparing to return to Nigeria to begin

work on a new novel when we talked about, among other things,
how reading Achebe convinced her that people who looked like her
belonged in books and the satisfactions of the writer's life.

⟨⟨⟨ ⟩⟩⟩

MARITA GOLDEN: You said in an interview that for your next book you were waiting for the spirits to come and speak to you. Do you feel that writing is intellectual as well as spiritual?

CHIMAMANDA N. ADICHIE: I think what I was trying to say is that there are times when in writing fiction I am not entirely and completely in control. I am not entirely conscious of making the choices I make. Sometimes when the writing is going well, I almost feel as though I'm high. And you realize that there's something else there. Sometimes I want to say it's a Higher Power.

MG: My husband's a musician, and we've had conversations about where his music comes from, and he always says he doesn't know.

CNA: Sometimes I'm just worried that it might sound a little over the top. I think also being Nigerian, there's a part of me that finds it's less appealing to talk about faith and God because in Nigeria people steal money and say we thank God, and people are horribly corrupt and say it's God's will.

MG: How has being a writer and writing the stories that you've written, which have been so painful and so difficult to write, changed you, enlarged you?

CNA: *Half of a Yellow Sun* was a difficult book to write. It was emotionally difficult because I was reading about all those things that happened during the Nigerian-Biafran War, and I realized my grandfather died during the war and I would sometimes imagine what my parents went through. It could have been me if I had been born a few years earlier. So it was deeply personal and emotional. I had the opportunity to tell the stories, to remember it for everybody else. What has been most rewarding is when I go back home and there are people who come up to me and sometimes cry and sometimes tell me that because of my book they're able to talk about what they went through, or they're able to tell their children things they have never talked about before. Really it's the most humbling thing. I sometimes stare at these people and I feel at the same time very big and very small.

MG: How does living in both places, Nigeria and the United States, affect your writing, going back and forth?

CNA: I think I'm just more aware of how much I'm an observer everywhere that I am. I find that sometimes it's good to have the opportunity to get away from home. I think also it makes me see Nigeria in a different way.

MG: How so?

CNA: When I'm at home, in Nigeria, I guess my world has become one in which I'm always making comparisons. So the last time I was home for Christmas and somebody was very sick and then they died, I remember thinking, well, the person was in the midfifties, so relatively young. And I thought they would not have died if they had been in another part of the world with access to better health care.

MG: What prepared you to tell these stories of war and political turmoil? Was there any inkling when you were younger, that you would grow into a storyteller? I know you said in one interview that your father wasn't particularly crazy about you being a writer.

CNA: I think it wasn't so much that he didn't want me to be a writer as it was that he and my mother in the beginning just wanted to make sure that I would do something that would make it possible for me to earn a living. It was go to medical school, become a doctor. You can always write. But I have to say that my parents are remarkable people because when I decided to cease the study of medicine, they said okay, which shocked me because I was expecting a huge fight.

MG: You grew up in an academic environment, so looking back with the benefit of hindsight, how did that prepare you to be a writer?

CNA: I've always been surrounded by books. It was just the norm that one read books. I feel that I was meant to be doing this writing, but I also think that I was fortunate to have the opportunity to fall in love with reading. And I think there are some amazing writers who didn't fall in love with reading as children just because they might not have had the opportunities I did. We had a fantastic children's library.

MG: Was it at the University of Nsukka?

CNA: Yes. I would go to the library and I went to the primary school, the university primary school. I owe everything I know today to that school. I had books and wonderful teachers. Very early on I think they could tell that I was very keen on books, and I was encouraged to read. Other children only had one book taken from the library; I'd take two. I fell in love with books.

MG: You read Chinua Achebe's *Things Fall Apart* when you were ten?

CNA: I wasn't normal. I was a very strange child. Again, this is the kind of thing that I have come to recognize only in retrospect now that I look back as an adult. But when I was much younger, I loved children's books, and I was in love with the idea of England. When I started to write, I was writing books where everybody was White, and they all lived in England.

MG: Now when you say when you started to write, how old were you then?

CNA: I was maybe six.

MG: So when you were writing your earliest stories, they reflected a colonized mentality?

CNA: Yes, and of course I didn't see anything odd about this. It's fascinating to me now. It was not until Achebe that things changed. I got the book from my friend's father who was a professor of English. My father was a professor of statistics, so we didn't have a lot of novels and literature in our house. My friend's father was a professor of English, and they had a fantastic library. So that's where I got the first copy of many books that I read. Achebe made me see that I could be in a book. Then I just went out looking for more books like it. Right at about the same time I read *The African Child* by Camara Laye and both books affected me so much. I absolutely loved them. And I realized I can be in a book. Those two books, more than any others, helped me to see that it was okay to write about people like me.

MG: So reading gave you a larger sense of the world?

CNA: Yes, and it helped me to make sense of the world.

MG: Are your books and the work of other contemporary African writers taught regularly in schools now in Nigeria? I know writers like Achebe and Wole Soyinka are.

CNA: The curriculum is still very heavy on the Achebe generation. I think it's a very good thing, but again I should say that it's not as bad as it used to be. I think that a child today interested in reading is more likely to find herself in a book now than in the 1980s.

MG: Education and reading are so intertwined, so interdependent, what do you think young people should know about the two that they don't?

CNA: That if you can't read and write properly, then you simply have not been educated. Both help with social skills and your ability to navigate the world, in and outside the work environment.

MG: You've been able to connect readers all over the world to your specific experience as an Igbo woman, as an African.

CNA: I think reading stories about other people makes us realize how they are just as human as we are. We may be different in culture and race and class, but we all have similar human needs and desires.

MG: You began writing your first novel as a senior in college, and that seems incredibly ambitious.

CNA: Actually it was the second novel. When I first wrote

it, it was really bad (she laughs). I had made the conscious decision that I wanted to be published and I wanted to know how publishing worked, and so I went to the library and I looked through the *Literary Market Place* to find agents, that kind of thing. I educated myself. And then I looked at the bookstore, and I realized that immigrant fiction was apparently a good thing to do. So I wrote this really horrible book, which was very derivative of a Chinese immigrant novel I had read. Basically I just had Nigerian characters instead of the Chinese characters. It was awful. I wrote that first and then realized it just wasn't going to work after I got maybe twenty rejections. Then I thought to myself, why don't I just write what I care about and then see what happens? Writing was a given. I would always write. I think the choice that I made, the conscious choice was that I wanted to be published, and writing and being published are two different things.

I think reading stories about other people makes us realize how they are just as human as we are.

MG: Oh definitely.

CNA: I would have been writing anyway. Even if I hadn't been published, I would still be writing. But I really decided that I wanted to be published and I wanted to make it happen.

MG: When did you start writing with serious intent?

CNA: When I began seriously thinking about publication

was when I first came to the U.S. and was attending Drexel University. I started to write short stories, and started to think seriously about becoming a writer. I had written a play while I was living in Nigeria, at sixteen, that was published by Spectrum in Nigeria. It was called *For Love of the Diaspora*.

MG: But then when you went to college you majored in Communications, and History, and Political Science. Why?

CNA: I didn't want to study English. I felt that it would get in the way of my creativity. I knew a little bit from taking literature in secondary school that the way that books are approached in an academic format just did not work for me.

MG: What is your critique of how they're approached?

CNA: It makes you think as a critic rather than as a creative person. I don't read any critical work. I don't want to think that way.

I want to fall in love with the book. I want to feel in addition to thinking. I want to feel that I can just immerse myself in the book. I don't want to keep thinking, and often in these classes you find that people attribute to writers things that writers themselves are not aware of. I once went to an academic conference where people were talking about my work, and I remember thinking, oh, I didn't realize I had all of those symbols in the text. But on the one hand I realize people need to make a living. People need to study these things. But it's just not for me, and so I really sort of avoid it.

MG: How do you like teaching creative writing?

CNA: I like it. It depends on if I'm allowed to teach a book I care about. At Princeton, I had my class read people they would never have read. I had writers from Martinique, and one of my students said, oh, I didn't know people in Martinique wrote fiction. And I said, well, they do and now you know.

MG: Do you find that your students read much in your creative writing classes?

CNA: Actually I think probably not. They read the work they are required to read. There's always the one or two bright students who want to be writers and who read, but on the whole, no. At Princeton I had really, very educated, very eager students, but when I wanted to talk about what they read outside of school and books they loved, there was always sort of talk about the movies. When I mention the book they would say, oh, there was a movie of the book.

MG: I'd like to talk a bit more about Chinua Achebe. It's one thing to read Achebe, but what does he give you as a writer?

CNA: Mostly what he gave me and what he continues to give me is a sense of a past. I think in Nigeria that what we need to do more in our education system is find ways to teach pride, because we don't. I'm watching my nephew, my American nephew, my sister's child, and the ways in which his education is based on these comforting myths about America, myths about the goodness of America, the greatness of America, about how America helps the world, about how America is always the good guy. I don't think a lot of the colonial education that we inherited gives us any sense of our present. And it didn't tell very much about our past either. So basically the story we received is that we lived in darkness until the good, kind White people came. I have many friends, for example, in Nigeria who are quite educated but who learned about the kings and queens of England going all the way back but don't know about their own past. Achebe does not capture the real gender complexities of the past—the position of women in precolonial Igboland was more complex than is shown in *Things Fall Apart*—but at least his books inform me that I had a real and a complex past.

MG: But he was writing at a particular time where issues like feminism and racial consciousness weren't part of the public discourse.

CNA: Yeah. Also maybe he just didn't know. Here was a young man who was the son of an Anglican minister, so maybe he didn't know. But really for me what it does, it gives me a sense of the past that refutes the characters that Joseph Conrad writes about. The characters in Achebe's books walked out in society in their own way, and they understood it, and it was complex. So that for me is much more than a good story.

MG: Is there a book that you read over and over?

CNA: Achebe's *Arrow of God*.

MG: What is it about that book?

CNA: I don't know actually. I just love it. I love the main character.

MG: I think that really in some ways that book may have been his most sophisticated work. But of course he's known for *Things Fall Apart*.

CNA: I think *Things Fall Apart* is easier, and I think it's less likely to confuse all these kids in America. But also there's something about it that I sometimes find myself feeling a little uncertain about. I'm not so sure I'm very pleased at the African books that these kids read.

MG: Why?

CNA: Because when I first came to the U.S., I had room-mates and they said to me, oh, you don't look African. They have certain contemporary stereotypes that sometimes makes me uncomfortable because I don't think people make it clear to them that a book like *Things Fall Apart* was set in a period one hundred years ago.

Unfortunately all these kids seem to know about Africa is the image that it's a place where somebody is starving or a man gets a machete and wants to cut off somebody's head.

MG: I'd like to talk about your research for *Half of a Yellow Sun.* How does one research a book about a war like that?

CNA: I read a lot of books. I tried to read almost every-thing that's been done about the war, but really just to get a sense of it and know the facts. To get the truth of it, I talked mostly to my parents. I talked to relatives and my parents and friends, but in the end I really depended on many memories and stories from my parents, my father in particular. I think my mother still finds it difficult to discuss. As I would read something, I would say to him, what do you remember of this, because I just felt that I didn't want this book to be about facts. I wanted to write about how people understood what was happening, not necessarily how the factual thing was.

MG: Very often in the writing of a book, you're struggling with it for a long time, and then there's a moment that you know that you've broken the back of the material, and that all the writing from that point on will be clear and dead on. What was the point for you with this book?

CNA: I think this book was a struggle from beginning to end. It seriously was, I was tortured until the end.

MG: Well, it was a glorious struggle.

CNA: I'm saying this in retrospect. When I was writing the book I was compelled. The book had been in my head for so long. I thought to myself my grandfathers are watching, that kind of thing. But at the same time, it was hard. It was really hard. And when I finished it, I thought I'd be very happy, but I wasn't. But after four years of writing, I guess joy came when my father read it, and he said to me, I knew this would be good; I did not think it would be this good. And it meant so much to me.

MG: Would you trade being a writer at this point in your life for any other career?

CNA: No. Because writing is the one thing that I truly, truly want to do, and feel that I have to do, and the thing that makes me happy, and the thing that gives me a sense of fulfillment.

CHIMAMANDA ADICHIE RECOMMENDS

Things Fall Apart Chinua Achebe

The African Child Camara Laye

Arrow of God Chinua Achebe

One Hundred Years of Solitude by Gabriel García
  Márquez

WIL HAYGOOD *is a national correspondent for the* WASHINGTON POST. *He is also a commanding literary craftsman. An award-winning journalist and biographer, Wil Haygood's first book,* THE HAYGOODS OF COLUMBUS: A LOVE STORY, *is a memoir that combines a coming-of-age story with a commentary on the seismic shifts in the social history of Black America.* TWO ON THE RIVER *is a book of lush and vivid photos and text chronicling a two-thousand-mile journey down the Mississippi. But Haygood yearned to take on big stories and larger-than-life men, narratives of those he calls "crossover people and rebels." With his biographies* KING OF THE CATS: THE LIFE AND TIMES OF ADAM CLAYTON POWELL, JR., IN BLACK AND*

WHITE: THE LIFE OF SAMMY DAVIS, JR., and SWEET THUNDER: THE LIFE AND TIMES OF SUGAR RAY ROBINSON, Haygood is recognized as among the first rank of contemporary biographers. The biography of Sammy Davis, Jr. won both the Hurston/Wright Legacy Award and the Award for Nonfiction from the Black Caucus of the American Library Association.

We talked in the study of his Washington, D.C., apartment. The walls of the room were filled with diagrams outlining the research he had done and outlines of the chapters he was writing for his then-in-progress biography of the great boxer Sugar Ray Robinson. In a conversation punctuated often by his deep, boisterous laughter and observations on the lessons and opportunities of his writing career, Haygood recalled his circuitous route into journalism and writing, the stories that have affected him most deeply, and how growing up in a house with several generations was the perfect training ground for a career as a writer.

MARITA GOLDEN: So much of your journalism in many ways celebrates family, and I want to begin by asking you how did the very nurturing environment of your childhood, where you were essentially raised by your grandmother and grandfather, prepare you to be a writer and a storyteller?

WIL HAYGOOD: My grandparents were very influential in my formation as a writer because they were unlettered. They did not go to junior high school even. They came to Columbus,

Ohio, from Selma, Alabama, and so, the fact that they were not writers almost meant that everything that they conveyed to me was oral, so there was a lot of talking. I think being in a household with my grandparents, my mother, and my older siblings, there was always what you might call "family drama," going on.

MG: You had several generations under one roof.

WH: Several generations living there. In any given year, an uncle who had lost his home might move into the basement, for instance, or my Aunt Creola who needed a place to stay for two or three months might move into an empty bedroom or just sleep on the couch downstairs. And my grandfather's brothers, when they came from the South, north to Ohio, they all brought shotguns because they were hunters in the South, and so, I got to hear Black men in their fifties and sixties sitting on the back porch, talking about rabbit hunting and these kinds of things.

MG: So, it was a very rich environment. With a lot of contradictions and complexities.

WH: Oh yes, there were people who drank, there were people who smoked (laughs), there were jack-leg preachers, there were women who did strange things out in the streets that nobody wanted me to know about. So it was an environment that lent itself to a little boy's mind always being alert and remembering.

MG: Did your grandparents tell you oral history stories about the family?

WH: No, but they were bringing other people into the house who told me things about their southern upbringing.

MG: Were you a great reader when you were a kid?

WH: Definitely. I'd hold on to words like a mountain climber hanging on to a side of a mountain. I realized early in life that words could take me to other time zones, other states. At about the age of eight or nine, I subscribed to magazines, fishing magazines mostly because I loved the idea of somebody in another state typing my name on a piece of paper and printing it on the magazine and that magazine coming right to the mailbox addressed to me. It was a fascinating thing to me that words sailed through the sky and had landed on my bunk bed, and it was like, whoever sent them, in my mind, only had one customer and that customer was me and their mission was to make little Wil Haygood in Columbus, Ohio, happy that he is now reading words about this fabulous trout stream up in Michigan.

MG: Did you go to the library much?

WH: I went to the library almost every day after school because I was fascinated about being around books. Just fascinated, and plus, libraries were free. There was no admission. You can go to the library and just read and sit and read, and I just knew that being in a library meant something to my soul and because, no matter how full of pain or sadness my day might have been, I knew I would be a little happier once I went to the library on North High Street in my hometown.

MG: Yes, I find that for a lot of writers, there's a division in our souls where we are drawn to the external world; we're extremely curious about that and there are questions and puzzles that we want to solve, yet we're drawn to reading and writing because traditionally they're solitary activities and being in solitude feeds us in different ways.

WH: Right, it does, I think. My twin sister, Wanda, often tells people, "Even when Wil was in the fourth and fifth grade, he would look at *Ebony Magazine* or *Newsweek* magazine and he would see somebody in a suit and tie, and he would say, 'I want to be just like this person.'" Magazines and the newspapers gave me a real sense that I could escape my surroundings someday, and not that my surroundings were out of Charles Dickens. It was just that reading gave me a sense of adventure. The ideas and lives of other people from books helped me move past the fear and anger of my brothers and sister. I read my way into opportunity. The more I read, the more I realized the world was big and I could find a place in it.

MG: What were your most beloved books as a child?

WH: I begged my mother to let me subscribe to the *Time Life* book series.

MG: What was the *Time Life* book series?

WH: It was like a big book about the State of Michigan or a big book about how to build a house. These hardback books would come to me monthly and I don't think she realized that they were the best toys that I could ever get. There wasn't money to always buy things for the kids on the weekends downtown, but if I could come home and there would be a box with a book in it in the living room for me, that was just awesome, that was special, that was unique.

MG: How did reading prepare you for your future?

WH: You know, in this sense, I think it gave my grandfather an indication, "Okay, I've got several grandsons, not all are doing well in school but every time this boy brings home his spelling test, he's got two or three stars on the top of the page, which meant an A." I got straight As in spelling and I did very well in English. I didn't do so well in science or math. So, I started to focus more on the things that I did well at; English, spelling, writing, and it was about that same time that I realized that you could do something—well, I sort of guess this came in about high school and then, going to college—I realized that you could convey a whole world of thoughts and sensations in a letter, because I came from a house where you only made a long-distance phone call under extreme emergency circumstances.

I read my way into opportunity. The more I read, the more I realized the world was big and I could find a place in it.

MG: Because they were expensive.

WH: Because they were expensive. And so, when I went to college in 1972 at Miami University in Ohio, I wanted to share this dazzling experience I was having. So I would write two or three letters a week for my family members back home. And I would put all sorts of things in my letter, like, what it was like to walk across campus at night, the sound of birds in the adjacent forest. Hueston Woods was a big forest in

Oxford, Ohio. I would write about certain teachers and what I thought about them.

MG: What books in college affected you deeply?

WH: I had a great teacher, Mary Musgrave, who was one of the few African-American professors at Miami University of Ohio. I took her Black literature class and we read James Baldwin's *Notes of a Native Son*. That book became important to me because it made me realize that you could read a book for more than just studying it and passing a test. I really read the book deeply and found that Baldwin's background of poverty and churchgoing mirrored my own. It was a book that related to me on a profoundly personal level.

MG: What did reading that book give you that stayed with you?

WH: As a writer, you want to feel that you're charting new ground. That what you're doing is original. James Baldwin's writing voice was original; we have never seen anything like that. Hemingway's writing voice was original; we have never seen anything like that.

MG: You have to go where no one else has gone before or is willing to go.

WH: Exactly.

MG: What got you into journalism? Why not fiction writing or poetry? How'd you come to choose that as a career? Or do you feel it chose you?

WH: In a way, it chose me.

MG: But it took a while for you to go into journalism, right?

WH: Yes. I came out of Miami University in Ohio with a degree in Urban Studies and worked a few odd jobs on the social services hotline, and then at senior citizens center. I wanted to write. My job at the social services agency, as a volunteer coordinator, was about to lose funding, and so I realized that I would need a job, and so there was a little Black weekly newspaper in Columbus, Ohio, called *The Columbus Call and Post,* and I went down there—very stern editor, Amos Lynch, and anyway, after going through a series of meetings, I got the job. That was my first paid writing job. I thought it was amazing. I thought it was just wonderful (smiles at the memory). I really had no training in journalism, but Amos Lynch and others on the newspaper said to themselves, well, he's got a way with words; he can write. They said that I could tell a story. That was important to me. The job only lasted about seven months because I just couldn't live on a hundred and five dollars a week even in 1979, so I quit. My grandfather was astonished. "How can you quit a paying job?" he asked me. And I thought I might turn to acting. I went to New York City. I caught a bus to New York City in 1981. I really couldn't act.

I applied for the executive training program at Macy's department store, was accepted, and lived in Brooklyn.

MG: How long were you with Macy's?

WH: For about a year and a half, then I was fired. I was an assistant manager in the Domestics department at the Queens branch of Macy's. I was sending out for towels, transferring towels and stuff. But, I used to walk around—this was the year that *The Short Stories of John Cheever* came out. It had a big orange cover. It was about six-hundred pages (laughs and shakes his head at the memory). I still have that book. I walked around with that book and took it into the stockroom when I should have been out on the floor organizing things, but since I was in New York, I thought that I needed to read stories about Sutton Place in New York. I read John Cheever, I read Langston Hughes. I read all these writers, and then, it was like, the more I read, the less of an image of a hard-charging executive I was conveying to upper management.

MG: What did you love about Cheever?

WH: I've always admired elegance, in fashion, in music, and the language in his books is always so elegant. Even when the stories are about misery, lies, deceit, they arc so beautifully written, and it's as though you can hear champagne glasses tinkling and soft music playing in the background. The beauty stands up. Among my favorites of his are *The Wapshot Scandal* and *Falconer.*

MG: So then, how'd you get into journalism?

WH: Well, I went back to Columbus and I said, "All right, Wil, you're twenty-eight years old. You really need to focus your life. You really need to find a career path, something that you love." There was nothing that I loved more than that seven months that I had a job as a journalist at the *Call and Post* as a feature writer and a sports editor. I look back on that, even as hard as it was, with as little money as I made, I look back on it with great fondness because I was writing and I really love to write.

So, I sat down at a manual typewriter in my bedroom at my grandfather's house and I typed out about fifteen letters to newspaper editors around the country, and I sent one to Ned Chilton, who was the publisher of the *Charleston West Virginia Gazette*, because the *New York Times* did a story about Ned Chilton being a very progressive newspaper publisher. Mind you, I had never in my life stepped foot in Charleston, West Virginia, but writing, words had given me the incentive, always explore, always take a chance, always strive.

MG: And he hired you?

WH: He did. As soon as I hit the newsroom, there's only one other Black there, a gentleman by the name of Edward Peeks, and he was the first person that I had met in my life who had written a book.

MG: What was the book about?

WH: It was a book about Martin Luther King, Jr., and the Civil Rights Movement. Peeks covered King for the *Baltimore Afro-American*. He took me into his study, and I about melted. This elegant man said, "Young Haygood, you might like to take a look at this little book. I daresay, Mr. Scribner published it himself; that would be Hemingway's publisher, as you know." He and I go sit in his study at his home, leafing through his hardback book with his name on it, and I wanted to yell out to the world, "See? It's possible! Somehow, I have landed within inches of a published author, published by Scribner who published Hemingway himself."

MG: And a Black man.

WH: Right. And a Black man, Edward Peeks. He was the only other Black on the staff.

MG: Did he become a mentor?

WH: I would definitely have to say yes. Because on the copy desk, as you know, all you have the opportunity to do is edit newspaper stories, but I come out of a writing frame of reference in my mind and I immediately—I had Tuesdays and Wednesdays off—and I immediately would scour the city with my notebook and find stories. I wouldn't be paid for these stories, but I would bring them back to the office.

And then, I would write editorials about Reagan's economic plans for poor folk, and the "safety net" was a big, big thing then, and so, Ned Chilton loved my editorials and he printed them, too. So here I was, writing editorials and the occasional feature story, and only getting paid for the copyediting, but I knew I was a writer. A friend once said, "Writing is, kind of like, a lawn and you have to mow that lawn all the time." You can't not write and call yourself a writer. So, even though I was on the copy desk for eight hours a day, I knew I had to write to train myself, to learn what I didn't know, plus I wanted to get out of there. I wanted to go someplace and be a writer.

And so, at the end of a year and a half, I had sixty-five editorials and stories that had been published. So, I went to the editor of the paper and said, "I've done all these pieces on my own time and I now would like to be considered for a job as a writer on your staff." He flat out said, "No."

MG: Why?

WH: He just told me that I was valuable on the copy desk, but to me, that seemed like he was trying to squash my dream to write. I was heartbroken.

So I went home and I did what I did to get to Charleston. I picked out a couple of newspapers and I wrote to John Craig, who was the editor of the *Pittsburgh Post-Gazette* in Pittsburgh, Pennsylvania.

MG: You were at the *Pittsburgh Post-Gazette*, then you went to the *Boston Globe*, a paper that had a reputation as a "writer's paper" because of the quality of the literary journalism many of its staffers produced. What were some of the stories you wrote there that mean the most to you?

WH: I will have to say being in South Africa before Mandela was released and apartheid was still on the books and having some of the African National Congress, the ANC people, sneak me around at night to meet ANC rebels who were still underground. That they would risk their lives to meet me at this house in Soweto to tell me about what it was like when they were young and Nelson Mandela was a lawyer in South Africa in the forties or fifties.

MG: What was it, their courage, their bravery that affected you so much?

WH: Yes, and it was also the realization that in my writing I knew that I had to somehow convey that these people, even tired, old, were still heroes. I had a sense that Mandela was going to be released. We all did. We did not know when, but I said, "When he is released, on the day he is released, I want to have a big story ready to pounce in the paper, you know, of him walking out and then looking back, with authentic voices." That's what I worked on for about three weeks. So on the day he walked out of prison, on the front page of the *Boston Globe*, we had this big piece that I had written. It was about three thousand words long, about Mandela's heroic past. You know, that meant a whole lot to me just being able to do that. I mean, I'm the guy who was cut from the high school basketball team twice and talked his way back onto the team. So, whenever I got a chance to write a story that blazed a trail in some way, wherever the paper wanted to send me, I knew I wanted to go.

(At this point Wil shows me the original *Boston Globe* article about the South African freedom fighters, which is quite long and accompanied by photos of the men he profiled.)

WH: Well, that's a story, isn't it?

MG: That it is. We are having this conversation at a watershed moment in the history of the press in America, a time when reading overall seems to be declining, if you believe the statistics, and there is some debate about that.

WH: Well, I think people are really torn. The more gadgets and channels on TV we have, the less time we have to read. So many of my college-educated friends have no library and I'm afraid of the answer I would get if I asked them what they are reading. I'm not sure what the answer is to this but I like the idea of book clubs and because we are such a celebrity culture, maybe some of the national arts organizations or the Hollywood producers could sponsor authors visiting schools.

MG: Reading and writing had such a positive impact on you as a student, at a fairly early age. How would you change the way various subjects are taught to stress their importance, as you said, beyond passing a test?

WH: Well, I think, for example, if Dr. King's legacy is

discussed, it would be important to talk with students about the books that influenced him, to make the connection between these epic lives and the books that were important to them.

MG: What has your writing career given you?

WH: Writing has been my attempt to unravel some of the hardships in my past life. My mother was an alcoholic, my father was separated from my mother a month after I was born, divorced, you know, family members in prison, family members who were on and off drugs, all my life, you know? So, I came with a whole lot of turmoil in my stomach, a lot of pain because there was always drama going around. A writer can kind of be an inward-looking psychiatrist, almost, trying to go back, trying to assess the damage, trying to look for the light at the end of the tunnel. I think about all the experiences that I've had and meeting all the wonderful editors, newspaper editors, who gave me a chance to find my writing voice. And then those who encouraged me to write books, Phil Bennett at the *Washington Post,* the managing editor; Len Downie, the former editor—they love the fact that I write books, that some of their journalists write books. Because I think that the books add to the journalism. The journalism adds to the books, even though they are two different muscles. A writing muscle is sort of like a parachute. You can put that thing on your back and you can float off anywhere.

MG: You have established yourself as a premier biographer. What is it about that genre that appeals to you?

WH: It is exhausting. It just zaps you. It is an interdisciplinary field, you know; when you're writing about the 1940s, the 1950s, the 1960s, you're writing about social events, you're writing about cultural events.

MG: Not just the person, but you're writing about their times.

WH: Right. And you're writing about every thread, in a way, of the history of this country. So my biography of Sugar Ray Robinson is not just a sports book. It's a book about Black businessmen in Harlem who couldn't get loans at the banks so Sugar Ray had to devise a way where he could own several buildings and turn one of them into a nightclub that became kind of a cultural center in Harlem, where New Yorkers would come to his club.

French stewardesses traveling to New York came to his club; Dizzy Gillespie, Miles Davis, Elizabeth Taylor, Richard Burton all hung out at his club. So within this book, there's another miniature book about Sugar Ray's nightclub, about a place where you could walk in the door and the walls of segregation would fall away.

(Wil shows me a wonderful large sepia-toned black-and-white photo of Sugar Ray Robinson and Sammy Davis, Jr. with their wives, sitting at a table in Robinson's nightclub. Dressed in the elegance of the period, the men and their wives are the picture of sophistication and glamour. Wil is beaming with pride and satisfaction as we discuss all the stories the photograph tells.)

MG: Of the three men that you've written about, you said you chose them specifically because one was a politician, one an entertainer, and one an athlete. Which one surprised you the most and which one did you admire the most?

WH: Sammy Davis, Jr. surprised me the most.

MG: Why?

WH: Well, because there was this image of him out there in the world, definitely in the USA, that he didn't have any backbone, that he didn't have any courage, that he was kind of a tool of Frank Sinatra. But the deeper I looked, the more I found out that he was really brilliant, that he had a lot of nerve and verve, that he took these two aging vaudevillians, his father Sammy Davis, Sr. and Will Mastin, and he stood them up and he said, "Follow me. We won't become extinct. I'll make sure that you have a living. That we will all have a living."

A lot of people thought because he had a White wife, May Britt, that he didn't care about Black folk, and then comes my interview with Harry Belafonte, who relates to me that our secret weapon in the Civil Rights Movement was Sammy Davis, Jr. He was one of the few Black folks who, if you needed twenty thousand dollars to bail a bunch of people in Mississippi out of jail who were arrested during a march, Sammy would wire the money the next day, and that story had never been told. Sammy fascinated me the most.

MG: What biographies or biographers are on your must-read list?

WH: Oh, goodness, Robert Caro. For the Lyndon Johnson books. I think David Levering Lewis's two biographies of W.E.B. DuBois are great; David Halberstam, the journalist and biographer who recently passed away; I think Edmund Morris's two biographies of Theodore Roosevelt are great. I love Gail Buckley's book about her mother, *The Hornes,* and of course Taylor Branch's books on Martin Luther King, Jr.

MG: What would you like your literary epitaph to be?

WH: Lost Worlds. I'd like people to say, "Haygood has written a book about a man we hardly knew." That means a lot to me. It means a lot to me in the Sugar Ray Robinson book to write about that sepia world. I think it is just as important as Gertrude Stein and Hemingway sitting around in New York. I think it is just as relevant to the history of this country to explore Lena Horne and Joe Louis and Sugar Ray Robinson sitting inside Sugar Ray's nightclub in 1947. I think it is just as important if you want an honest portrait, you know, of where America was in that time period.

I am just drawn to these cross-over lives, these people who crossed over, who were rebels. Maybe the larger society did not want Sammy or did not want Adam but they pushed through anyway; you know, they said, "Here I come. I am coming. I'm coming down the road and if you have good ears you ought to be able to hear the hoofs of my stallion that I ride because I won't be turning back." I am fascinated by that.

MG: And you did those lives so much justice. Last question, are there any books that you read more than once or that you go back to for something important?

WH: Two books that I think are just rich in texture and sweet are *Elbow Room* by James Alan McPherson, the book of short stories, and Robert Caro's *The Power Broker* about Robert Moses. Caro started his writing career as a journalist on the staff of *Newsday* and that encouraged me, made me feel that I could cross the road and write in another genre and be accepted if the books were good.

MG: Wil, your books are much better than good, they are great.

WIL HAYGOOD RECOMMENDS
(Because They Are About America)

Lush Life by Richard Price

When Harlem Was in Vogue by David Levering Lewis

Dreamer by Charles Johnson

The Power Broker by Robert Caro

NIKKI GIOVANNI is a literary

icon whose poetry and prose has spoken with urgency and lyricism
to readers for forty years. She is a writer who was present at the
birth of the Black Arts Movement and one of its primary creators.

Born in Knoxville, Tennessee, in 1943, Nikki Giovanni grew
up in Cincinnati, Ohio, and, with her sister, returned to Knoxville each summer to visit their grandparents. Those summers in
Knoxville, her years attending Fisk University, from which she
graduated with honors, and the political consciousness of her proud
family gave Giovanni the themes that she continually explores
in her work. The present and past historical experience of Black
Americans, its grace and power, despite a brutal legacy of slavery,

segregation, and disenfranchisement is the essence of Giovanni's oeuvre. Her poems, which combine the skill and sophistication of a master poet with the inspiration and healing power of a Black liberation preacher, have spoken to generations of young people reading her work not only for its artistry but also for its promise that all things are indeed possible.

Among her best-known works are GEMINI: AN EXTENDED AUTOBIOGRAPHICAL STATEMENT ON MY FIRST TWENTY-FIVE YEARS OF BEING A BLACK POET, THE WOMEN AND THE MEN, EGO-TRIPPING AND OTHER POEMS FOR YOUNG PEOPLE, *and* A DIALOGUE: JAMES BALDWIN AND NIKKI GIOVANNI. *And her recording* TRUTH IS ON ITS WAY *is a perennial best-selling album of gospel music and poetry. Giovanni is also the award-winning author of several books for children.*

She is a beloved member of the faculty at Virginia Polytechnic in Blacksburg, Virginia, where she has been a Distinguished Professor since 1987. Giovanni's poem "We Are Virginia Tech" rallied the spirits of the school and the nation in the aftermath of the massacre of thirty-two students at the school in 2007.

Nikki Giovanni is the author of nearly forty books, the recipient of scores of honorary degrees, and has won several NAACP Image Awards for her books.

MARITA GOLDEN: When did you know you were a writer? And why poetry as opposed to another genre?

NIKKI GIOVANNI: I know I'm a writer because of what I continue to work on. One morning I'll wake up and there won't be a leftover poem. You know you're a writer because you're always writing.

MG: Why do you write poetry?

NG: Every time we celebrate we turn to poetry, and every time we mourn we turn to poetry. I think poetry is pretty big.

MG: When you were growing up, I'm sure there was lots of support in your family for your writing and reading. Could you talk about that a little bit?

NG: Well, I came up in a family of readers, and particularly my mom was a reader. One of the first gifts my father gave my mother when he was courting her was *A Bell for Adono* by John Hersey.

MG: What were you reading as a child?

NG: I have half a shelf at home of my old books, and one of my favorites was the Mother West Wind series by Thornton Burgess. My grandmother was a terrific influence.

MG: Was she a reader?

NG: Oh yeah. Grandmother was from Knoxville, Tennessee, and she would get Reader's Digest Condensed Novels.

MG: I read those as a teenager. Oh god, a whole education through those condensed books.

NG: I also remember, as a child in Knoxville, going to the Gateway Bookstore, and it was one of the few places in a segregated city that I could go into no matter what. I couldn't go into a theater. I couldn't go to amusement parks. I would go by and look in the window and see what the new books were. The first book that I ever bought was *Clarence Darrow for the Defense*.

MG: How old were you?

NG: Ten or eleven.

You know you're a writer because you're always writing.

MG: So the libraries were segregated?

NG: Oh, they were, but still I went. I remember the time I asked Mrs. Long, the librarian, for *Leaves of Grass* by Whitman, and she was like, okay, I can probably get that tomorrow or the next day. I had no idea what that woman was going to have to go through to get that book for me. I wrote a poem that's in *Acolytes* about the incident. People could be incredibly cruel to Black people. They would give her the book because they were obligated to lend the book, in a library. But they could have asked who wants it. But she went and got it, and said, Nikki, here's your book. And so I'm reading Walt Whitman.

MG: At what age?

NG: I was about twelve, because I read Walt Whitman and Alfred North Whitehead about the same time. And so she had to go get Alfred North Whitehead, a theoretical man that's always interested me.

MG: I know you're aware of the discourse about the decline in reading; do you agree with that assertion?

NG: I think that we're selling people on the fact that

people don't read. But I've watched the *Harry Potter* phenomenon. People were bitching and bitching and bitching, kids don't read. And yet right here in the New River Valley, where you could literally put hundred-dollar bills on your body, go naked down the street, and somebody would say, Ms. Golden, you don't have any clothes on, and those are hundred-dollar bills, right?

A place where we just don't steal but yet *Harry Potter* ultimately had to be kept behind the counter. The book was being stolen by kids because their parents wouldn't buy it. The school libraries were having trouble because people were saying it was witchcraft. I knew I was going to be an important writer when Louis Micheaux, who owned a famous bookstore in Harlem, said to me, your book is being stolen from my store. I said, that's it, I'm going to make it, and I knew it. When people steal books, they feel the book is important. *Harry Potter* was being stolen.

That said something about reading. There's a genre of books called Street Lit, which is just a racist label, I think, and people say, well, we know they're not well written and all that, but they're books. What makes *Gang Girl* any less relevant to its time than *Pride and Prejudice*? So we want the kids to check out *Pride and Prejudice* but not *Gang Girl*. I do not understand. Zane tells a good story. E. Lynn Harris told a good story, and E. Lynn Harris is read by people who are busy. E. Lynn sold those books through beauty parlors.

MG: And out of his trunk.

NG: I know he got the out-of-trunk idea from me. The first Christmas gift as a grown person my sister gave me was a hand cart because I used to carry books around. That's the way you do it, and if I hadn't been able to make other changes, that's what I'd be doing. But I could earn a living.

MG: What about required reading when you were a student?

NG: When I was growing up, there were a hundred books you should have read to go to college. I finished that off in like the ninth grade. It's just like, okay, this is what I have to read, so that you can pass all of these exams. Some of it was enjoyable, some of it wasn't, but it's your job so you get it done.

MG: But clearly you loved reading; why?

NG: Reading allows you to see the world in a new way. We can't go back to the days of past history but we can be part of history by reading. The kids today who read are mostly in high school. But I read to my students in class, I read to them out loud.

MG: How do you encourage reading in the context of family life?

NG: I think reading together with your children is important. It makes a difference.

MG: Do you operate from inspiration or curiosity as a writer?

NG: Curiosity. For me the constant question is why and why not? I think if you're not contradicting yourself, you're not interesting.

MG: You've received so much recognition for your work, what does that mean to you?

NG: I'm honored to touch people spiritually.

MG: What books have most affected your work and your life?

NG: Without a doubt, the work of Gwendolyn Brooks, Langston Hughes, and Paul Laurence Dunbar. Books about science, space. Toni Morrison's *Sula*. I liked *Song Yet Sung* by James McBride a lot.

MG: Are there any books you read periodically?

NG: *Medusa & the Snail* by Lewis Thomas, it is a great science book that is about everything.

MG: The young poets and the hip-hop folks are doing some great stuff in terms of literature and writing.

NG: I was down in Greensboro for a literary festival, and the group that opened it, they were welcoming me with poetry. So first you had the little kids doing it, and they were so cute. But then when the teenagers came, a kid read a poem, "Not on My Watch." He was just naming atrocities and after each event, he said, "Not on my watch." Then he brought it all the way down to slavery. It was beautiful. So the young kids are reading. Nobody just likes how they're delivering.

MG: What advice do you give to aspiring young poets?

NG: I really do everything in my power to avoid it. People don't need advice, and that becomes kind of a game, like people don't need role models. Like people don't need mentors. We know people don't need mentors because Langston Hughes didn't have a career until he got rid of his.

I watch the little things. I think any time a writer looks out the window, there ought to be something. There ought to be something he sees.

MG: If you could meet any writer from the past, who would it be?

NG: Lorraine Hansberry, she's one person that I've always wanted to meet. I would love to have met her. First of all, she was extremely smart. And it's not that I don't like other people. I do. But she was very smart, and she was very courageous. All of her career, Lorraine stood for something. And in her courage, she had balance. So when we look at *A Raisin in the Sun,* we're still looking at a courageous statement, but she's not going to cop out. She didn't punk the Blacks off, and she didn't excuse the Whites. But you could see both points.

MG: Do you want to name the favorite book of yours that you've written?

NG: I'm always into the next book.

MG: So you do really believe your favorite book is the one you're writing now.

NG: Yes, but I'm very proud of everything, and because I'm a poet, I reread my work. I carry it. I can go back and realize, oh, I haven't read this section of that book. It's like if I haven't read "Nikki Rosa" in five years. It's fresh. Of course, *Ego-Tripping,* it's a very big sampling for me, and so I do read that all the time. And of course I'll never read "We Are Virginia Tech" aloud again because there's no point. You can't do that. But being proud of it and being pleased with what you've done and rediscovering your own work, it's not so bad. You're really happy with it. But I'm always into the next thing.

MG: You're always into where your bicycle is going to take you.

NG: It's kind of fun because one day somebody will ask

me this question, and if I'm lucky I'll be sitting someplace like this and I'll answer, and then I'll know that I have completed my reign.

NIKKI GIOVANNI RECOMMENDS

Sula by Toni Morrison

The poetry of Gwendolyn Brooks, Langston Hughes, and Paul Laurence Dunbar

Song Yet Sung by James McBride

Medusa & the Snail by Lewis Thomas

Acknowledgments

I WANT TO acknowledge the generosity of the writers who talked with me about our shared passion for reading and writing. They have each given the world much through their work as dream weavers. I thank them on behalf of the many lives and spirits they have touched. I also thank my editors Alison Callahan and Cory Hunter and especially my original editor Janet Hill who was always a good ally and friend. As always, my husband Joe believed me through this as he does with everything I do.

ML